SEEMS LIKE SMOOTH SAILING

A memoir on the realities of working on a cruise ship

by

Sam Catling

CRANTHORPE
MILLNER

A CIP catalogue record for this title is available from the British Library.

First published (2020)

ISBN 978-1-912964-24-6 (Paperback)

www.cranthorpemillner.com

Cranthorpe Millner Publishers

Contents

Introduction

First of all let me kick this off by saying I've been lazy. I need to admit this to myself and to you the reader, as I've made a lot of excuses and let myself get away with it for quite some time. Basically I went into a depressed, reclusive state for about two and a half years where I achieved absolutely nothing. During that time my most overbearing thought was that I did not matter to anyone, and therefore why should anything I have to say matter to anyone either. Not much happened in those years; a lot of long blank stares and empty days. A lot of us have probably been in that place where we think, *what's the point anymore?* and it can take some time for us to get out of that destructive mind-set.

For me, having focus and concentration is a daily struggle, as I have adult attention deficit disorder (ADD). This does not mean that I have an unrelenting surplus of energy, but rather that my mind is operated like a remote control in the hands of a restless teenager who keeps flicking from one channel to the next. The moment I managed to stop channel surfing happened to me on my first day of university in 2014. I had just turned 27, and therefore a mature student by definition. On the very first lesson of the very first day, my very first lecturer asked the class to write a very mini-autobiography and gave us ten minutes to do so.

It's amazing how such a simple thing like that can really help your brain reactivate, like a dusty old spaceship control station booting up for the first time in decades because a crew mate finally awoke from hyper sleep. I was steering rudderless for so long and had been at war with myself for what felt like an eternity. I'd made a few feeble attempts to write some sketches and comedy songs for no other reason other than to try to cheer myself up, but until now no-one had ever asked me to write anything about myself before (*well not since I was back at school, so it had been a while*). To me, this made a huge difference because it was like having someone who was there to listen all of a sudden, whereas before all my writing had come from a place of abandonment. My internal monologue would always bully me into thinking that no one would care, I wasn't special or original and I shouldn't even bother ... that old chestnut.

I hate to start the book in this way - by giving off a negative first impression. I really don't like the idea of getting all serious right from the beginning, but, I think for the purposes of this book, and it being my very first one, I feel it's important to be up front and honest with you about who I am/was. I'd like to get the heavy stuff out of the way early doors so that we can all relax, proceed to break the ice, and go on to have some laughs together and take it at our own pace.

Back in the classroom at uni, I put pencil to paper and rapidly scribbled everything I could say without stopping. I could practically smell the lead starting to smoke. I churned out a full autobiographical page in less than five minutes, and instantly felt like a huge weight had been lifted off my shoulders. Why hadn't I done this before? Why did I need to be asked to do this by someone else so that I would end up doing it? Then a young lad of about eighteen/nineteen approached me (in fact most of the class were of a similar age, I was the old man of the group and much closer to the ages of the lecturers themselves). He commented on how I must be really good at writing because I'd completed the task so quickly. This basic level of flattery was immediately followed with a request to help him out with his. My internal response was, *I don't know your life, kid,* but to have responded in that way would have gone completely against my moral code as I genuinely do like to help people. So I asked him a bit about himself, work, family, you know, the standards. He said he had been working at a petrol station for a while and they tried to make him an assistant manager. He didn't want to fall into a career of this kind, declined the offer and instead enrolled at university. It sort of reminded me of that scene in Fight Club where Brad Pitt is holding a gun to the head of Raymond the service station cashier, and pretty much forces him to go to veterinary school otherwise he'll kill him. Except in this scenario I wasn't

Brad Pitt in possession of a loaded firearm, and I wasn't being anywhere near as forceful with my line of questioning. I smiled at the lad and said, "Wise choice, what about your hobbies?" to which he replied, with a look of sorrow and what seemed like regret, "Okay ... but you have to understand something ... since I was thirteen the PlayStation 3 has been out ..."

Now I haven't owned a games console since the PlayStation 2 which was some time ago because we're now up to the PlayStation 4 (well, depending on when you read this. Let's just say the PlayStation X). In my lifespan computer games have gone from the primitive 8-bit graphics to whatever high def virtual reality hoverboard/hamster wheel harness super tech we're up to now. I struggled to find empathy for the lad's response because to me it was a lame excuse for not having an active hobby, although there are many people who would argue that gaming is definitely a hobby and for some even a career! I'm not arguing with anyone, I'm just letting you know that it looked like he had remorse residing in his retinas. A regret for probably playing far too many video games and for not being able to say something cool like he was into scuba diving or gymnastics. Why those are the first two hobbies that came to mind I do not know. I've never really done either of them except for a bit of snorkelling and tumble tots when I was a kid.

Anyway, the year I started to actually write this book was towards the end of 2017, which should give you some idea of how bad my ADD is. Since finishing university I have worked on this book and other writing projects, held numerous jobs, become a handyman, a film extra, and have just generally been living life.

Oh and I went and got myself married to Sujin from South Korea in January 2017, and just in case you're wondering, South Korea is the good bit.

I know it's kind of terrible of me to say, but that young lad who had difficulty in writing anything interesting about himself gave me a second wind and my confidence back. He inadvertently struck a match that lit my passion for writing, because he helped me to realise that I actually have plenty of cool stories to share.

I'll do my best to stick to a linear timeline, but if it seems a bit fragmented, or jumps ahead in time then back again, I apologise. After all, I am writing this book over seven years after I finished working on-board cruise ships. We struggle as it is with specific details when trying to tell people about a dream we had, so to say this has been a challenge is an understatement.

At the time most of the events in this book took place I was a mere lad of nineteen and late to bloom. For whatever reason I was confident enough to get up on stage in front of a room full of strangers, but painfully shy whenever talking to attractive members of the opposite sex. So just in case you've heard on the grapevine a few squalid tales of debauchery that a life on-board can bring, I want to promise you early on that this is not that kind of book. That being said, it doesn't mean there aren't a few risqué moments thrown in here for good measure. However I tend to unfortunately be in the possession of a rather inconsistent charm-o-meter. Think Hugh Grant one minute, Mr Bean the next.

I never really kept a diary on-board because I was working seven days a week. As it was I struggled to even stay in contact with my parents on a regular basis so blogging was out of the question. In my later years working on-board, I would sometimes go around crew areas in my downtime with a notepad and pen, and interview fellow crew members for some of their best experiences from their time working at sea. I've been combing through old notebooks, emails, Facebook posts, pictures and talking to former colleagues to recoup the raw writing materials needed for this book.

This book is not a work of fiction, it is a gathering of true stories collected and told mainly for the purposes of entertainment, and no-one's real name other than my own has been used. None of what is written in this book is intended to offend anyone, these are mostly just my (and a few others') experiences from a time spent living at sea.

I've had more than enough time to reflect on my experiences, so really this book is me playing catch-up, taking stock of myself and trying to have something to show between the years of 2006 to 2010, and ultimately leaving something behind for others to enjoy.

There are many pros and cons to working on a ship which I'll get into in this book, but to summarise as briefly as I can: I count myself as one lucky sonofabitch to have had the opportunity to broaden my cultural horizons, and also be able to learn and grow in terms of confidence and maturity. It's an experience unlike any other. You can either make the most of it or just coast along for the ride dragging your knuckles as you go. Living on-board a ship can at times be like living inside a giant bubble, where the stresses and strains of every-day life back home cease to exist. Back on land after a contract, my newly found charismatic stage presence and extroverted nature was at times too much for people. Sadly this led me to feel ostracised from certain social groups. The knock-on effect of this was that I became overly self-aware, and I had too much charisma for my own good. So instead of just being able to simply dial it down a little, it completely switched off, and I withdrew into myself. I had no a face or voice. Now I've rebuilt the foundations of my confidence, I am able to stand on my own two feet and I feel capable to re-join the rest of society, being careful as I go not to tread on anyone's toes.

Throughout the process of writing this book, I have been reading a whole bunch of books written by other people who have also worked on cruise ships. Primarily I was reading them to help recall the things I had forgotten and so for that reason, they were really helpful, but I also wanted to see how my book could be different, figure out what my unique selling point was and where the gap in the market was. As no one person owns the monopoly for writing an account of their time spent at sea, I saw no harm in doing the same.

One of my hopes is that this book inspires guys and gals like that lad I met on the first day of university, to find their own voice, pushes them out the door to go and venture forth on their own journey of discovery, and maybe even encourages them to write a book of their own one day.

Also to the kid who said, "You have to understand something ... since I was thirteen the PlayStation 3 has been out ..." - don't be ashamed of playing games, man. I recently went to a friend's house and played the new Call of Duty. We were shooting up zombies on the fricking Titanic! It practically gave me a panic attack but it was a lot of fun!

The title of this book is my response to those who would assume that life working on-board is just an extended holiday. Whilst it may offer opportunities that give you the illusion you're on vacation, you're never truly off the clock. On-board and in passenger areas the name badge is to always be visible on your person, and when you're ashore you're never more than 6 feet away from a guest at any given time.

I definitely don't want people to see the cover of my work and think, *Oh god, not another bloody cruise ship book! I've read so many already!* I also don't want to repeat what others have already explained. Most of them did it in far greater detail, used a much richer vocabulary and described it in far greater poetic beauty. Those people were all overachievers anyway (probably), professional officers and managers, exceptionally skilled musicians and courageous dive instructors, whereas I go into my story a complete spring chicken, a blank canvas on a clean slate. I was just out of school and had no ideas of my own … I was an idiot. So with that, I dedicate this book to those who feel as though they have no real talent, no area of expertise and the people who are just along for the ride but try to make the most of it.

This book is for the everyman!

Hope you enjoy.

Sam

Chapter 1

Changing Course

It began just like any other wet blanket tell–all tale. I was just one of many hopeless teenagers out there, void of inspiration, bereft of ambition and lacking any testicles. Puberty decided it was going to take its time with me, and I was in danger of falling behind with not just my pubic hair, but also an increasing lack of my own self-confidence.

When I was in primary school I was diagnosed with A.D.D. In secondary school the diagnosis was re-confirmed, when I was college I was diagnosed with it yet again. At that point, for me, it was as if I was hearing it for the very first time, probably because whenever I had been told before, I most likely wasn't paying any attention.

I struggled through college and so after completing my A-levels I had no designs or aspirations whatsoever toward academic achievement.

I was working a part-time job as a trolley Wally at Asda, and for a very short period I also ground my teeth behind a desk for a telesales company. Neither gave me any sort of job satisfaction and for a few months, I was a real burden to my folks (sorry about that, guys). One evening in 2006 my nan came by the house fresh from her first ever cruise ship holiday. She was sun-kissed and glowing with excitement as she told us all about her voyage. As she rounded off her story she turned to me and said, "Sam, why don't you go and work on a ship?" At first, I thought she had sunstroke as I was certain I lacked any of the necessary skills needed to work in such a place. I'd once considered joining the Navy because I liked the idea of getting away and going out to sea, but the money was crap, the living quarters were tiny, and the only job description that I really leaned towards was the unfortunately titled role: 'Seaman Specialist'. With friends like mine, I'd never be able to live a quiet life ever again so I didn't persevere with a career in the forces. My nan however, informed me that there were young people around my age who worked within the entertainment team on-board. I leaned in closer and was keen to know more. She then told me how she had spoken to some of the ents about how they got started (that's entertainment hosts for short, not ents as in Treebeard and his other tree buddies from the Lord of the Rings). I listened to everything she had to say with newfound enthusiasm and she concluded by saying, "You'd be great at something like that!"

I wasn't particularly married to a career in telesales or the supermarket, so I followed up my nan's suggestion and advice by heading to the local newsagent and ordering a subscription to the Stage magazine. It was in the jobs section of this publication where roles were listed for cruise ship staff. Annoyingly, the first few copies advertised nothing that matched up to what I was looking for. It was after about three weeks that I found an advertisement for cruise ship ents hosts. I got so excited that I hurriedly submitted an email request for an application pack. When it arrived in the post I was buzzing excessively. In my mind, I was practically already dancing the Cha-Cha Slide on the open deck with the sea breeze caressing my face. Then I opened the envelope and read the first line at the top of the page on a list of questions …

What previous experience do you have within the entertainment industry?

Well my heart just turned to lead and sank. It took my whole body with it and I was now a man overboard losing the fight to stay above sea level. I snapped out of the daydream and back to reality. I threw the application across the room and let out a noise that can only be spelt, Mmwraaah!! I had no experience, who was I kidding? I'd been in education all my life and the only two other jobs I'd ever had were a waiter and publishing distributor (which is a fancy way of saying paperboy). I remember thinking, I wonder how else I am inadequately qualified for this job? So I went and picked up the application and read through the other questions. They were thankfully just standard questions that I was able to answer. I left the first one blank with the intention of going back to it, and when I did, I had a long hard think to myself. I re-read the question aloud in my head and put emphasis on different parts of the sentence in a variety of combinations. **What previous experience DO I have within the entertainment industry?** So I thought outside the box and conclusively decided it was best to write, 'I have had extensive experience working with trolleys in ASDA car park for the past two years'.

And that boys and girls is how I landed an interview to work on-board a cruise ship. They got in touch to inform me that my little tongue-in-cheek comment got a big laugh in the office, and would I be able to come in and meet with them for a chat. I was speechless. I honestly thought that I wouldn't be taken seriously and my form would just get thrown on the heap of unsuccessful applicants.

The actual interview was pretty informal. I got asked a bunch of questions about my home and personal life as they tried to size me up. I made them laugh a couple of times which is always good and we parted ways shaking hands. The drive there and back took just under eight hours, and the nerves of, *did I get it did I get it?* lasted the entirety of the return trip.

That evening during dinner I got a phone call from the interviewer. The call was straight to the point which was good for me because I was right on edge. The guy on the phone said, "Sam ... it's good news ... you've got the job." Unable to contain my excitement I let off a scream of pure elation directly into the phone. I probably damaged the poor guy's eardrums but I like to think he was used to delivering that kind of good news and had pre-emptively muted the phone line as quickly as he had told me of my good fortune.

Now, I do not wish to brag, because recruitment processes vary from company to company, but every entertainer I ever met always told me that they had to audition for their role, and I just had a one-on-one interview. In fact, every job I ever got onwards from my first contract was either through a phone-call interview or reference. Surprisingly the only time I ever didn't get a job was when I actually had to audition for it! I guess I'm just crap when it comes to that kind of pressure.

In readiness for the start of my first contract, I had to meet certain criteria. Firstly I would have to acquire an ENG1 seafarer's medical, then go onto a week of training at a maritime academy in Southampton. This would cover such topics as survival techniques at sea, crowd control management, basic firefighting and elementary first aid. I remember having the medical in Harley Street by a doctor who informed me that he had recently completed a medical assessment for none other than David Beckham! Although I am not up to the same level of fitness as Mr Beckham, I was cleared by the doc and given my certification.

The Maritime Academy was a strange place. It was mostly occupied by sickly looking teenagers who were sea cadets in training to become officers. I was informed that the flunk out rate for completing the sea cadet program was as high as 54%. A portly looking lad bounded up to me one afternoon and proudly began telling me all of the places he had been on the big cargo ships during his training. I asked which place out of all of them was his favourite, to which he replied, "Oh we weren't actually allowed to get off the ship, but when I grow up I'm going to be a captain!" He had a good attitude but I couldn't help but think he lacked the look of someone able to command respect and one to dish out discipline, let alone adhere to some.

My lodgings for the week were in a building that was up to par with a four-star hotel, not too shabby, I thought. And one evening as I stood outside the building having a cigarette, a squad of cadets came marching by, and in unison they halted, turned to face my direction and saluted me! It struck me as a bit odd but I deduced that it could have been for any of the following reasons - either they were just practising, they mistook me for someone else, or they were just very polite cadets. I then found out later from reception that there had been a mix up with my room. The lavish hotel style rooms where I was staying were designated for high ranking officers and captains, and so having no place among them I would have to move into cadet quarters. And who should my roommate be, but the portly lad from earlier that day, who as it turns out had a rather tumultuous tummy whilst we slept.

With me on the training course were a few other people all bound for different cruises so I wasn't totally alone. We spent the majority of our time in classrooms having to listen to a number of long lectures about the importance of health and safety at sea, and crowd control management (which is as about as exciting as it sounds). It wasn't all boring though. At one point I had to give CPR on a mannequin to the beat of Staying Alive by the Bee-Gees, which I'm told is the rhythm you need to keep to in order to do it properly, fun fact!

During basic firefighting we learnt about the different types of fire and how to extinguish them (something I've had to sit through more times than I can remember). We had to go into a simulated fire wearing the proper full body equipment, including breathing apparatus. Our mission was to go into this small building that came complete with its own remotely controlled fire, and as a team we had to put it out and rescue a dummy that was supposed to be the equivalent dead weight of an eight-year-old. Our teacher must have been joking because it weighed a metric tonne.

The most exciting thing we had to look forward to was the course on survival techniques at sea. We were given some idea of what to expect, which involved being dressed in wetsuits, learning how to correctly don a life jacket, and having to jump into a pool from a great height. (Pppph…easy). We also were told to expect strobe lighting, a wave pool and wind machines to simulate a full-blown storm at sea. Madness! I couldn't wait, it sounded epic, but the reality of the situation was that those things were at another training facility with better funding. Instead of the wind machine, there was a CD player with a stormy soundtrack. Instead of strobe lighting, there was a guy flicking the light switch on and off, and instead of a wave pool, another guy just stood in the pool and splashed the shit out of us! To be fair, it wasn't that bad a simulation.

At the end of the week, my classmates and I had to say goodbye and we wished each other well on our contracts. When I got home my mum was getting the suitcase out of the loft, and it was time to start packing. And by packing I mean - my mum did it all for me because it was the last chance she'd have for a while to be all mumsy. I was subjected to a barrage of questioning: *Will you need this? Shall I pack that? Do you have enough skin cream* (for my Eczema)? etc. I still had a week before I had to leave but mothers do like to worry, especially as this was the first time I was leaving the nest for more than two weeks.

When it came to the big day, it was all a bit emotional. My whole family had signed a card wishing me bon voyage and safe travels, nearly bringing a tear to my eye but I stayed strong and held them back. My mum, on the other hand, let the floodgates open. I was actually quite relieved when I got to the other side of the terminal because she was making such a scene. Anyone who might have been watching would have thought I was being deployed straight to the front lines. The reality of my situation was that I was flying to Gibraltar to jump on a ship and learn how to present gameshows.

One short haul flight and a bus ride later, I arrived at the dock which is when I got my first proper look at my new home for the next 6 months.

Chapter 2

A New Chapter ... Literally

It's a funny thing, standing toe to toe with a huge metal vessel. I was jaw agape in awe of her size. It's both teasing and tempting, daunting and inviting at the same time. Before I'd even set foot on-board so many questions and emotions ran through my head: was I happily scared or scared happy? Who will my boss be? What will the crew be like? Will I get my own cabin? If not, who do I have to share with? What will the food be like? Will there be girls? All pretty standard concerns.

The first obstacle to overcome was how I get on the ship. There was no gangplank. The ship was in dry dock which means there is no water beneath it, instead, it was held up by thick beams of wood. During this period the ship goes through general maintenance and refurbishment. A huge bonus to this was that I wouldn't have to go straight to work as there were no guests. I would have time to get to know the ropes and my fellow crew before diving in at the deep end.

I was instructed by a dock worker to get inside this metal cage with my luggage, which was then picked up by a crane and lifted on to the back deck of the ship. As I was being lowered I had to call out sharply to a crew member on-board, who was standing, of all places, directly beneath the cage. Whilst I trusted the crane operator's vision and judgement, I still felt a strong sense of urgency to get some communication across quickly. "Mate, get the fuck out of the way!" I called, and he did. So you might say I arrived on the ship in a gloriously spectacular fashion, but somehow I managed to take any grace and dignity and discard it overboard as soon as I descended on to the open deck.

My first impressions of life on-board were slightly skewed as everywhere and everyone was in refurb-mode. All the floors, furniture and fixtures were covered in white sheets, and all the officers and crew were stripped of the stripes on their shoulders and instead all wore the same plain white boiler suits making it impossible to know who was who. I felt like I had just stepped into the Wonka vision white room and was about to be shrunken down like Mike Teavee. A man, casually dressed, carrying a walkie-talkie, approached me and said, "Sam?" This was my ACD (assistant cruise director) Gary.

For those of you unfamiliar with the chain of command when it comes to entertainment, the CD (cruise director) is at the top of the pyramid, followed by the ACD. Then beneath that, it's fragmented into separate departments all of which have heads of department who report to the ACD and CD. Ent hosts, show team, kids' hosts, musicians and technicians make up the entertainments team on-board a ship.

As I walked with Gary through the ship I was nearly knocked for 6 by the potency of the paint fumes and feeling a little dizzy I had to go through the regular sign-in procedures, which involves dealing with paperwork at the purser's office. Once all that's sorted you get your cabin key, start unpacking and get yourself settled. Crew cabins on cruise ships are far more spacious than the ones you get on naval ships. On those, you would be looking at 6 to a room with two triple bunk beds, a drawer each and that's it! Luckily I was sharing with just one other, and if you aren't accustomed to sharing then perhaps a life at sea isn't for you. However, don't be under any illusions that the crew cabins are by any means luxurious, they're far from it. My advice - get down to IKEA and buy a few things to customise your space as it makes a huge difference.

My cabin-mate was a senior technician who seemed normal enough, right up until the moment when he proudly decided to show me his DVD collection, which was two large leather-bound books filled to the brim with porn. At that point, sharing a room made for 6 people suddenly sounded more appealing. With that being said he was respectful when it came to his favourite hobby, in the sense that he was good enough not to cum in my face. Night after night I would wake up to the sound of the bed above me creaking away. I was the youngest crew member on-board at the time and this guy was a <u>senior</u> technician, so rather than speak up and try to put an end to it, I thought life would be more bearable if I just let him finish. I'd put up with it by sticking my fingers in my ears, burying my head under a pillow and praying for a quick climax. I've always hated confrontation, and back then to have to confront someone about something as delicate an issue as masturbation was my idea of hell. These days I'm not quite so forgiving, and also these days we don't need large leather-bound books to keep all of our porn in one place, let alone two of them! Today everything is accessible online at the click of a button, but if the internet goes down, the trusty wank-bank isn't functioning properly and your girlfriend doesn't exist, what are you going to do!? You would have to I suppose be prepared for that situation with some kind of back-up, and for most people, an external hard drive provides the solution. I once met a guy who claimed (God knows why) to have a Terabyte of porn. Now to give you some idea of how much porn that actually is, you could fit approximately 500 hours' worth of movies onto one Terabyte. Assuming that each movie is roughly 120 minutes long, that's about 250 movies.

When asked about his collection and why he felt the need to hold on to that much of it, the answer was: "I like to watch it for the stories" (said no-one else I've ever met in my life before).

One of my first and most memorable experiences with porn was when a friend gave me a VHS tape to borrow. He told me that he'd found it in his parent's bedroom and before I could ask he assured me that it wasn't footage of his folks going at it, but rather a collection of scenes that had been recorded off one of those television X channels. He warned me that the first scene was a bit rough, but that it got better, and when I had a moment to myself I checked it out. The first scene was indeed a bit difficult to watch, as it contained an old man having sex with an obese red head in the woods with shackles, on a rainy day. I was met with a bit of a conundrum, because I didn't to watch the clip, but I didn't want to stop the video and fast forward past anything else that I might miss. So I had to fast forward whilst it was playing, which is the reason why I am still able to remember the scene in such vivid detail, because it's now burned into my brain, in fast forward.

I hid the video in a storage cupboard above my bed assuming of course that it would be safe. However I got home from school one day and shortly after I had gone upstairs to my room my mum called out to me and said, "Sam, could you come down here please?" She was standing purposefully abreast of the TV in the living room, arms folded with the remote in her hand. She said,

"I was doing a bit of spring cleaning earlier," (I gulped) "and ... well ... would you mind explaining this please?" She hit play, and on the screen came that classic clip of an old man having sex with an obese red head in the woods with shackles, on a rainy day. Just like when I used to rent videos out from blockbuster, I always wound them back to the start for the next person like a good boy. I nearly went to say, "But mum, it gets better!" but instead I protested my innocence. "I've never seen it, a friend lent it to me, I don't know what it is, oh God please turn it off!" She did just that, folks. The video was immediately ejected much to my relief, but then she lifted the cassette flap and started to pull the tape out, spewing, "Filth, absolute filth" as she went.

So basically ... if you remember once owning and losing a video of an old man having sex with an obese red head in the woods with shackles, on a rainy day, then my sincere apologies to you for not hiding it better.

Another time when I was in secondary school, I came across a rather sinister schoolboy in the playground one day. He emulated perfectly the classic coat full of contraband TV trope. I remember this lad sidled up next to me during break and without making eye contact softly spoke the words, "You wanna buy some porn?" He then opened up one side of his blazer to reveal a stack of CDs tucked inside his breast pocket. They were all freshly burned with various clips of pornography to meet the demands of the everyday schoolboy. Thinking back this was actually pretty ingenious. It was at a time when technology had just given us the ability to re-write CDs, and it was also a time when most people still had dial-up modems. So to have something that would save me the time of messing around with the family computer and soiling up the internet history, was nothing short of genius. I applauded the boy, for he had found his market niche and tapped into it. So I said, "One please", and that is the end of this rather derailing porn filled anecdote.

The tiny cabin bathroom took some getting used to. You could shit, shower and shave all at the same time if you'd have wanted. For the first few weeks, I was unwillingly forced into a rather intimate relationship with my shower curtain. I called her Denise. I tried playing hard to get, gave her the cold shoulder, even tried taking her down a peg, but the damn skirt couldn't take the hint; she was all over me and got really clingy! This was all too much too soon and things got a little hot and steamy. I'm a man who likes his space, so in typical fashion, I gave the old it's not you, it's me, we need some time apart, speech but she wasn't having it. Eventually a few weeks later I finally ended things because she went off the rails. So I did the only thing any self-respecting man would do, I washed my hands of the relationship and hung her out to dry.

Now ridiculous as that story might have sounded it isn't too dissimilar from some of the relationships I had with actual women whilst at sea. You live and work in the same environment as them seven days a week with no escape, and so two weeks with them feels like six months … but more on relationships later.

As this was my first time away from home I was happy to learn that there was a housekeeping and laundry service on-board. All crew cabins are maintained by housekeeping staff who came and cleaned twice a day, whereas when I lived alone my bedroom back home was lucky to be cleaned once a week! They also take your dirty clothes down to laundry and have them cleaned and pressed for you ready for the next day, and it was custom to always make sure to tip the cabin steward because those guys are some of the hardest workers I've ever met in my life. My mum never got a tip from me before, but making the transition from my mother doing my laundry to a housekeeper was a welcome change. It did however take a considerable amount of time to learn how to be independent and adapt to life in the real world without these luxuries post cruise ship career. Oh well, we've all got to grow up sometime.

Now because the ship was in dry dock for the first two weeks of my contract, there were no guests on-board which meant there were no duties as well. This made getting used to life on a ship (that wasn't at sea) a lot easier. I got to explore the ship in my normal clothes and sit at the bar without getting into any trouble. I was told I should take advantage of this, as once the guests got on-board, I'd never be able to do it again.

After I had unpacked a few essentials, Gary took me on a little tour of the ship. He introduced me to his boss, making him my boss's boss, the cruise director Stewart. We all sat in one of the bars for a nice little chat whilst having a coffee and a cigarette. The atmosphere was so relaxed I had my feet up on the table which was covered in a white sheet so I felt it was okay. No-one seemed to mind, then after a few minutes of getting-to-know-you chit chat, Gary leaned forward and whispered without moving his lips, "Sam, get your feet off the table." I didn't really hear what he said so my response was just, "Huh?" then Stewart leaned forward and said the same thing. "Sam, get your feet off the table." I must have had something in my ears or was still a bit out of it from the paint fumes because I didn't really hear what he said either. I then clocked that both Stewart and Gary's eyes were darting from side to side. So I looked behind me and a man in a white boiler suit was standing there. "Hello," I said cheerfully. Stewart cleared his throat and said directly in my ear "Sam … that's the captain." I jumped straight up and started to brush the space where my feet had been on the table. "Hello Captain, nice to meet you" now sounding less cheerful, and instead more servile and apologetic. It's fair to say that I never really was able to win that particular captain over for the rest of the contract. My first impression was so poor that he always had a dismissive attitude towards me from that day forward. Lesson one for anyone going to work on ships for the first time, the captain is basically God on-board, so always be on your best behaviour when in his presence and definitely don't say anything bad about him, as you never know when he might be standing right behind you.

My first day on-board was otherwise incident free, and because there were no guests on, it meant that I could settle in and get my bearings. I realise that since the beginning of this book I haven't really told you what it is that an ents host does. Well, that is because up until this point in the story I was pretty much as clueless as you. I had no idea what my responsibilities were, how above and beyond the call of duty I would later be expected to go, or how I'd need to be prepared for how many situations I'd find myself in where I would have to rise to the occasion. Gary would later introduce me to my senior ents host Karl, who would basically go on to teach me the ropes. There was a lot to get my head around in those first few days, learning all the dos and don'ts of the ship's rules, codes of conduct and the little grey areas that weren't policed to heavily. My duties to name a few included hosting events across a wide range of activities, such as sports tournaments for basketball, mini golf, table tennis, shuffleboard, darts etc. Hosting demonstrations for cocktail making, ice, fruit and veg carving, and towel and napkin folding. And yes that was a real activity which actually got huge turnouts on a weekly basis. Then there were ship tours, bingo, quizzes, karaoke, game shows and of course socialising. They actually put it in my schedule! It didn't matter that all my activities were already heavily social, apparently it wasn't enough, so between certain hours of the day, I would have to wander around the ship and approach people striking up random conversations just trying to fill the time slot, and nine times out of ten I'd be having the same conversation with the guests. The passengers on the more affordable cruises would repeatedly ask how I got my job, how long I'd been at sea and did I go to some kind of special stage school. On the more exclusive and expensive cruises the guests demonstrated to me that they really didn't care about any of that, they just liked talking about their favourite subject ... money. At first I really didn't mind being forced to socialise as it brought me out of my shell and introduced me to many interesting and intelligent people, but after a while I became fed up with it. So as soon as the clock struck the hour I was set to finish socialising, I would make up some excuse so that I could leave. Usually, I would fake an *Oh I just realised ...! I've just got to be anywhere but here!* Kind of moment, and then it was back to my cabin for a much-needed power nap, something I never used to do but quickly became an expert at.

One of the key areas I needed to gain proficiency in was public speaking. Karl would allocate a couple hours every day to educate me on the craft of live hosting. We covered such things as stage presence, etiquette, microphone skills and trying to curb my enthusiasm. It's fair to say that back then I was a lot gabbier, I would always be applying my own brand of childish whimsy to most situations. I remember the first time I was ever handed a live microphone. It was just Karl, my fellow ents hosts and me in a big empty lounge with no guests.

I was given a short, easy to remember speech to orate with full pomposity, and as soon as I said the first word into the mic I completely froze and shut down. Funny how such a small thing can render you utterly speechless. It was as if for the first time in my life I'd suddenly become fully aware of myself. I was totally blank as to what I was supposed to say, how to stand and where to look. To tell you the truth I just felt awkward, and like I was on the receiving end of some practical joke. Every day I would go through the motions of working a 360 stage to an imaginary 500-seater audience. The aim was to make sure I was confident enough to be able to run game shows to a packed audience by myself in just two weeks of being on-board. There were so many different bloody formats with so many ridiculous rules that I just couldn't get them locked down. I was getting so frustrated with myself for being so shit all the time that I felt like crying. I wanted so badly to be good at my job but found that hosting in front of a family audience takes a lot of practice and a think-before-you-speak mentality. A useful trick I learnt for using the microphone is to forget you even have it in your hand, and instead treat it as an extension of your arm. This puts you more at ease over time as you become accustomed to holding the mic up to your mouth and hearing it fill the room. The fear of public speaking, also known as Glossophobia, affects around 20% of Brits, and stats according to YouGov suggests that women are twice as likely to make up those numbers. The fear stems from the dread of failure, it's the looking silly in front of people that adds pressure to the act of public speaking, and is why to some the very idea of it can seem impossible. I didn't really care if I wound up looking silly, I was happy at that time just to be making people laugh.

Once I had battled away stage fright and the awkwardness it was time to tackle my delivery, diction, tone, modulation, pitch, inflexion, intonation, pronunciation and timbre. Basically put, my accent was the problem. At the time I had a tendency to speak with my native Essex accent with bullet speed quickness. When I was very young I had a problem with speaking too fast so my parents arranged for me to have elocution lessons with a lovely little old lady who I recall to be extremely dramatic. She taught me how to slow my speech down and to speak all proper like, init. Of course it had been many years since I had had this training, and so was now trying to recall those classes from memory to aid me in getting my lips around the words. I practised warming up my mouth with specific exercises and doing tongue twisters. To recommend a couple of my routine regulars, try repeating the classic - *Red lorry yellow lorry* or, *One smart fellow he felt smart, two smart fellows they felt smart, three smart fellows they felt smart and they all felt smart together.* My favourite, if I had to choose one, was a bit longer, but when I nailed it I felt and still do feel some small measure of pride. It goes, *she stood upon the balustraded balcony inexplicably mimicking him hiccupping whilst amicably welcoming him in.* Now that's a hard one! If you're reading with your inside voice and thinking nothing of it, then I challenge you to go back and try it out loud.

I had to learn to ditch the common Essex accent by tightening the screws and sanding down the edges. I didn't have as bad an Essex accent as some of those people on reality TV who constantly exclaim *Oh my god, Shu'up! That is well bad!* However, my superiors' concern was that I was still somewhat a bit <u>too</u> Essex for the general audience to understand.

The two weeks of intense microphone training was a good education to have, but like all education, it's one thing to learn about and another thing entirely to put into practice, especially when it comes to public speaking. When the time came on my first contract to see who would be hosting some of the evening game shows, my name was not on the list. As hard as I had worked I still was not fully competent or confident with this level of hosting, and after two weeks of speaking on a mic to an empty room who could blame me? I remember being a little disappointed but at the same time massively relieved. I would start this contract off by being in charge of the lighter side of the on-board entertainment which didn't require a mic - such as the sports locker (making sure it was neat and tidy) and hosting sports tournaments, also restocking the crossword and Sudoku puzzles and making sure the library was kept in order. Not being allowed on the mic at first did push me harder though. It gave me the opportunity to work towards something rather than just being allowed to do it straight from the off, and seeing how I had bypassed the initial audition phase I thought, fair enough.

Now because we were still in dry dock there is one significant detail that we as a team were able to take advantage of, and that was overnighters. During the day a ship stays in port and guests have the opportunity to go out and explore, and an overnighter is one of the rarest things to happen during a contract as a ship needs to get to the next destination for the next day. So if the guests aren't on the ship during the night then they aren't in the bars, restaurants or casinos spending money, and thus not making the company any money. For pretty much two weeks the team and I would explore Gibraltar's nightlife, which is mostly just English style pubs and sports bars. I didn't know anything about Gibraltar at the time, all I knew was that it was British owned and they spoke English. However, being in another country I always wanted to try and do my best to speak a bit of the lingo. So I would approach the long-haired Spanish-looking bartender and do my best to order "Cuatro cervezas, por favor," and the usual response would be along the lines of, "Wassat you want, four beers? Yeah, sure no worries mate!" Turns out these guys were more cockney than me!

It was nice to be in such good company and doing a job that I really enjoyed for once. During the first two weeks of training there was an evenly balanced mixture of hard work and leisure time. One day we were allowed the afternoon off to go on an excursion, so we got into a minibus and were driven up into the hilltops which overlooked all of Gibraltar. When we started to hear the noise of tiny feet scrambling on top of the roof we knew we were close to our destination. Five minutes later we were out and about with the monkeys which are local to that area. Cute yes, but these really are the most devious little bastards ever. Honestly, they would pickpocket tourists' wallets, they'd steal their food, and I saw about five of them sitting in a row all tossing off looking like a group of hairy bell ringers, dinging their dongs merrily on high indeed. The drive on the way back down in the bus was one of the scariest things I have ever done, and I've jumped out of a plane! I was sitting in the passenger seat next to the driver who was going full speed through a narrow alleyway down-hill approaching a T junction. The driver looked at me and said, "Which way mate, right or left?" Not having a clue but being desperate for him to decide before it was too late I just panicked and said "Light! No, reft!" He said, "Wrong! It was secret answer number three - the hidden alleyway!" He then made a sharp obtuse angle right-hand turn that made us go back on ourselves down an even tighter road. He assured us that it was okay, as everyone drives like that in Gibraltar, which of course made us all feel much safer.

Back on-board all things health and safety related are the responsibility of the health and safety officer. These officers are in charge of making sure all crew were properly educated when it came to understanding the ship's various code words for things. Obviously, if there is a fire on-board no one would be stupid enough to make an announcement to the guests about it as it would start a panic and have them running for the lifeboats. By using the public address system you can alert the firefighting team to their post without the guests being any the wiser. The health and safety officer would also make you sit through long, tedious lectures on what fire needs to thrive, and how to use a fire extinguisher, stuff I'd already covered a few weeks ago. It didn't matter, I still had to go through it again, and in a few weeks' time, I'd be going through it again. These lectures were compulsory for all crew, and after a week of them we would have to take a test which we needed to pass otherwise we would be sent home.

I was more than just a bit nervous, but everyone reassures you, *oh it's easy, you'll pass it no problem*, but until you have actually done it, and been told that you've passed, it doesn't really make a blind bit of difference what people tell you. So every spare minute I got I was ploughing through handbooks on safety procedures, trying to make sure that my newfound career wasn't over before it started. I honestly put in what felt like a much more thorough and focused study effort than I had for my GCSEs and A levels. When the time came to sit the test I was like Arnold J. Rimmer from Red Dwarf, no I wasn't covered head to toe in crib notes, but I was so nervous I was practically shaking and deliriously dizzy. Then as soon as I opened the paper I was able to breathe a sigh of relief. It <u>was</u> easy! Questions so easy a newborn baby could probably pass, like what colour is fire, and multiple choice - if you see a fire should you (a) Dive in head first, (b) Run away screaming but tell no-one why, or (c) Pull the emergency fire alarm and evacuate the area?

I raced through the test as quickly as possible so I could go back outside to play. I know if you are reading this now and are about to take a similar kind of test that people tell you is easy but are still nervous about, then this passage is a bit redundant because of course, you will still be thinking to yourself - what if I fail!   We all get like that, we all like to worry, but the kind of questions we were given were on things we'd gone over so many times it was almost impossible for any individual to forget. All the same, I'd still say make sure you study just in case years from now the tests get harder and this advice becomes outdated, which I guess applies to all tests but you probably already knew that didn't you.

There are three different types of people that work on-board. I'm not talking about the philosophical motivations of people, I'm referring to their titles. There are officers, staff and crew. The rules for these three vary from ship to ship but basically, the officers get a lot more benefits that do not extend to anyone else, and of course they all get their own cabin. The staff normally share two to a cabin, get to be in passenger areas and can drink with the guests (within reason). They are also allowed to eat in some passenger areas and if invited by a guest or have family visiting on-board, they can eat in the fancy restaurant as well. The crew are not allowed in passenger areas unless it is their job, such as waiters and bar staff etc. They are only allowed to eat in the crew mess, drink in the crew bar and usually share anywhere from two to four to a cabin. I felt very fortunate to be in the position I was in right from the beginning, as I had seen the food on offer in the crew mess and was quite quick to schedule my meals up on the lido. This was far better than the mess but worse than the fancy restaurant. The only problem was if the lido was full of guests, then we would have to give them priority and take our chances in the mess. Another problem I would later discover is that because there are guests there, and because I'm such a wonderfully friendly and engaging person to be around, guests would always come up to me mid--meal. Now I don't know if you are anything like me when you're hungry, but I am one of those people that just likes to eat and be left alone. I'd be about to put the first forkful into my salivating pie hole, and on regular occurrences, I would be abruptly asked a question by a guest or worse joined by them. You might think I'm being a bit of a diva but some guests just do not respect crew's need for personal space, and as for the stupid questions that they would ask whilst a full spoonful hovered centimetres from my agape mouth, I think I will have to save a chapter for them later on in the book. I'll give you one for now just to keep you wanting more. The following is a mash-up of queries compacted into one infuriating conversation.

Guest: Excuse me, what time is the midnight buffet?

Crew: Err. It's at midnight

Guest: And where is the buffet?

Crew: It's on deck nine forward in the restaurant

Guest: What floor would that be on?

Crew: It's on deck nine

Guest: How will I know I'm on deck nine?

Crew: There will be Nine Signs visible to you across the whole deck

Guest: Do you mean there are just nine signs across the deck or are there many signs that say, Nine?

Crew: I'm sorry, yes, there are many signs that say, Nine

Guest: Okay, and how do I get there?

Crew: Just press number nine in the lift

Guest: Right ... and where are the lifts?

Crew: At either end of any passenger cabin corridor

Guest: And which lifts go up and which go down?

Crew: (*Face-palm+ sigh*) They all go up and they all go down

Guest: Great ... and sorry, remind me, the buffet starts at ...?

The only night of the cruise when we could eat uninterrupted on the lido was when it was formal night. All the guests would dress up in their penguin suits and posh frocks and eat in the fancy restaurant. It was on this night the crew pulled out all the stops and presented the guests with something they called The Buffet Gala Magnifique which served up all kinds of delicious looking grub. The centrepieces that always really set off the display were the ice sculptures and the fruit and veg carvings made earlier that day. Unfortunately throughout the evening as the buffet went on, the ice sculptures would melt and start to look really sad, and fruit and veg carvings would attract the odd fruit fly. The crew also made these little fruit and veg models, like a tiny car with courgette chassis, or an owl made out of orange and melon. People would pick away at them as they went past until you eventually had something that looked like an abomination of nature, as if it had come from Silent Hill.

On formal night one custom is that guests will queue up around the block to meet the captain and have a photo taken with him. It's not an obligation by any means, more a compulsion. They figure it's something they may as well do just so they can say they met him or her, and also because most of them can't wait to ask their really funny question: *Wait, if you're here who's driving the ship?* Which is funny the first time you hear it but once you hear it on average twenty times a cruise it wears a little thin. Guests would be so pleased with themselves for making that joke that they would go out of their way to find me and re-tell the story all over again, adding every bit of detail and emphasis they could think of to elaborate just how their meteoric rise to comedic genius was finally realised. "Here, Sam, you'll never guess what I said to the captain last night." I'd play along and say, "I dunno ... what?" "I said, aren't you supposed to be upstairs driving the boat? HAHAHAHA!" I made every effort to make it look as though it was one of those stories that naturally caught me off guard and incited genuine laughter, but inside I would be fuming. It's bad enough that they've brought this story to me under the assumption that they invented the joke, but worse even still is that they called the ship, the cruise, the vessel, or even liner A BOAT! We used to say that a boat is something you get into if there is something wrong with the ship. ALSO! You don't drive a ship, you sodding well steer it! I should've been a teacher but somehow I don't think I've got the required level of patience for that role.

Everyone due to start work as soon as the dry dock was over was now on-board. The whole team was in place and ready to go, though for some reason we had not one but two full show teams and ents hosts on-board. Normally when a team has reached the end of their contract they get flown home, but on this occasion the previous teams were kept on to help make changes and repairs to the costumes and sets for the shows.

Having two sets of entertainers on at once is so the transition of teams is seamless, and there isn't a noticeable drop in the standard of entertainment for the guests. So when we waved goodbye to Gibraltar it was a quick trip over to Palma de Mallorca for the start of the first cruise. Obviously, it was great to have two teams of attractive female dancers around and getting to see the live West End style shows and game shows in action was a real education. I was also given new exposure into the world of men who bat for the other team. Practically two-thirds if not three quarters of the entertainments team was a friend of Dorothy, and by contract's end they all wanted me to be her friend as well.

Being from a small town in Essex I had literally no encounters with homosexuals before this time, so it took some adjusting to get used to the flamboyancy and invasion of both ear and personal space. The naïve, young me though all gay men were loud and flamboyant, so when some of them told me they were gay I was amazed as I'd had no idea. Then of course there were the guys who were so camp I did wonder how they even functioned back home in the real world. I made it quite clear early on that I wasn't going to join the club, and that I would be okay with the banter but that's as far as it would go. For the most part they respected my wishes and knew when they had gone too far, on another contract further down the line however, I wasn't so lucky, but more on that much later.

The first time I ever took part in a sail away deck party was an experience I will always remember fondly. It was a clear, starry night with a gentle cooling breeze circulating the open deck. Two teams of entertainers up on the open deck were singing their hearts out and dancing like wildlings around the pool edge. The band were in full swing, and all the guests in attendance were waving their arms in the air to sing-along classics as the ship pulled away from port. Glasses clinking, hips twisting and bodies popping. The vibe was juicy, the atmosphere was succulent. Not a single negative thought ran through my mind, and if it did it couldn't have brought me down from the high I was on. The captain sounded the ship's horn and cheers from the crowd filled the air. It was perfect. As the ship swept through a milk pond and out to sea I got a tingle of excitement that ran down my spine as I realised I could definitely do this for a while.

Chapter 3

Making My Mark

As I wasn't going to be hosting anything anytime soon I was eager to work hard and earn my place among my peers. I stayed the course and worked at keeping the sports locker, library and prop cupboard tidy as often as I could to score some extra brownie points, but then I would inevitably lose those points when I'd have too much to drink in the crew bar and make a fool of myself (we're all young once!*)*. On one occasion I was dared to take a large bite of an aubergine that was way past its sell-by date. Ten Euros was the prize for completing the challenge and to give you some idea how bad it was, it was wearing its very own lustrous fur coat fit for any formal evening. The skin was extremely tough and it took some serious effort to puncture it with my teeth. As I tore through its rubbery exterior I got a huge mouthful of gooey green putrid flesh. I was encouraged by others to hold it down, chew and swallow my way to victory, because the caveat was that if I was sick I didn't get the money. However the sensation of chewing food that was tougher than old boots and smelt worse than them to boot was unbearable. So I ran for the nearest railing and launched it overboard retching loudly. To make things even worse the whole event was captured on camera which then circulated throughout the crew rather quickly, so from that day on I made a conscious effort to drink less. I was nineteen and, being from blighty, the peer pressure to drink started when I was fourteen. Back in those days my friends and I would give money to older lads to go and buy our drink for us and there was no problem. At fifteen we got a bit cockier and started going to pubs, we actually managed to find a few that never checked our ID and assumed we were of age. So my drinking tolerance wasn't all that bad, but it was definitely going to be tested to the limits when guests with all-inclusive drink cards would constantly offer to 'buy' me drinks.

It quickly became known that I was the youngest crew member on-board, and as a result this endeared a lot of the guests and crew to me. Not a week would go by where I wouldn't get some random woman offering to play the role of my on-board surrogate mother. I don't know why this kept happening, I guess it's because I possess the look of someone only a mother could love, or maybe it's because they would all just love to have a son like me :) By nature I am not what anyone would call a mummy's boy, and actually I was often reminded to call home when anyone would ask me about my family and if I missed them. I think I went two or three weeks of my first contract without ever calling home. I had sent a couple emails but was yet to actually call. I had been so busy with my duties and adapting to life at sea that I had totally forgotten.

I remember it was the New Year's Eve fireworks display in Madeira 2006. The realisation that I hadn't spoken to any of my family for the two or so months I'd been away hit me like a tonne of bricks. The firework display surpassed my expectations so much that I was overwhelmed with emotion and I began to miss home. There must be a strong psychological link in my mind that inherently connects firework displays with my family.

One of my earlier memories from childhood is when I was around six or seven. I recall it was the fifth of November, bonfire night, and Mum had made spaghetti Bolognese for dinner. I was being an extremely fussy eater which I was notorious for back then, and I was yelling and throwing tantrums at the table: "I don't like it, I don't want to eat that". Mum would try her best to keep her cool and get me to finish using child mind logic. "You don't have to eat those tomatoes but you do have to eat your carrots"; "if you eat half your onions and half your mushrooms then you can leave the table"; "if you finish another four mouthfuls I won't hit you again!" (I'm joking, I'm joking! It was only two mouthfuls). I used to be so bad at eating that my mum would have to re-heat my food at least three times because if it was too cold I wouldn't eat it either. I was being such a brat on this occasion that I was made to sit with my food on my lap in the kitchen on this random wooden three legged milking stool that we had (we didn't have a cow, but we did have a milking stool …). The humiliation and isolation of this punishment sent me into a flood of tearful hysterics. I didn't like my food and sobbed through waterlogged eyes, spacing every word on an in breath: "I. Just. Want. To. Go. To. See. The. Fi. Er. Works". That's when my mum lost it. She picked up my plate and shouted, "THATS IT!" and upturned it directly onto my head. With my new look spaghetti wig I went into a state of shock. The tears subsided and my face became expressionless. Then my mum instantly felt guilty and took me to see the display. She recalls the events of that evening somewhat differently, however the point of this story is that to this day, I have never been fussy with my food ever again, so thanks, Mum!

I think more than anything the display in Madeira just triggered the feeling that I wished my family could have been there to share the experience with me, and the more I thought about them, the more I thought about how much I loved and missed them. So along came the waterworks, and like all personal matters on-board it wasn't a secret for very long. A colleague was kind enough to lend me their mobile and I called my mummy and blubbed to her down the phone. *I. Miss. You. And.*

Ev. Ry. One. At. Home. To my recollection I can honestly say that I've never been as homesick as I was at that moment. When my mum picked up the phone, she answered cheerfully, almost too cheerfully for my liking. I could hear what sounded like a party going on in the background and she was clearly having a good time. I remember being upfront with her about missing home, the family and my PlayStation (The old one I had years ago remember?). To my surprise her response was a very casual and slightly disinterested, "That's nice, dear". Clearly mum was enjoying the liberation that came with my absence from the family home, and she was enjoying life to the fullest. So I sobbed a heart-felt goodbye and hung up the phone.

This event helped to shape my on-board persona for the next few months, as it was now out in the open that I was an overly sensitive mummy's boy away from his family for the first time. I was given the catchy macho nickname 'Sammy boy' and it stuck for longer than I would have liked it to. I went on to ships to find myself and learn how to become a man, but wound up getting put into a stasis chamber of boyhood instead.

At the beginning of every cruise was embarkation day, and at the end of every cruise was debarkation. The debarking guests get off in the morning and the embarking guests arrive in the afternoon. Sounds simple in theory right, but every ship and every port is different and guests love to make it as difficult as they can for you sometimes.

It's an early start for debark as there is a lot of people traffic to manage and a lot of questions and complaints to assist with. Being that the job on-board is seven days a week, the window of opportunity to go ashore and have some proper you time is situated between the old guests leaving and new guests arriving. So when the old guests are trundling down the corridor with their luggage saying goodbye to everyone, stopping and starting to make sure they have everything, in the back of your mind is a voice repeating the phrase, *Get off Get off Get off* ... This internal mantra goes undetected for the most part and is what motivates the crew's teamwork on these mornings. The quicker the crew pull together as a team and get the guests disembarked the more time we would have off that day.

In my early days of cruising a week went by a lot slower as everything was still new to me, and during that time I forged a lot of connections with the passengers. When it was the end of their holiday I actually felt quite sad to see some of them go. Every cruise ended with people crying as they said goodbye to those who they had bonded with. Holiday romances were now coming to an end with the individuals promising to stay in touch, which we all know never happens. All this emotion up in the air was by no means a one off, it was weekly. As the weeks went by from the start of my first contract, I gradually developed thicker skin and I began to put up an emotional brick wall. No longer did I get choked up whenever guests had to leave, instead, I learnt to accept that there were no goodbyes really, as there would be another 1000+ guests coming to replace them later on that day.

With the exception of families coming on-board there are three types of people who go on cruise ship holidays. Crew commonly refer to these types as newly-weds, over-feds and soon-to-be-deads.

The soon-to-be-deads would spend most their time doing crosswords under a towel on the open deck, or by playing shuffleboard and bingo. If they weren't doing either of these three things then they might also be waiting down at reception each morning for the newly printed crossword and Sudoku puzzles. Heaven forbid you should be a couple minutes late in providing them, as these types of passengers take their puzzling seriously, and if by honest mistake you brought up puzzles they had already completed then you basically got lynched.

The over-feds were hard to miss, literally, and I'm sorry to have to write that the number of them sky rocketed when I later started working on American ships. They weren't always over-feds though, as the old saying goes on ships, 'Come as passengers, and leave as cargo'. To be fair who can blame them, food was on the go 24/7 and for a lot of people eating as much as you can is a great way to spend your holiday.

As for the newly-weds, to be honest we didn't really see much of them once they got on-board and went to their cabin. The captain would often reply to guests' concerns about the rockiness of the ship, by using them as a scapegoat: "Don't worry, we just have a lot of newly-weds on-board this week"

I don't like to generalise guests as being stupid but at times there were so many of them asking ridiculous questions it was hard not to. One evening at the end of a cruise I overheard a guest ask at reception, "Do I put my luggage outside the cabin before or after I go to sleep?" My answer to that question would be before, definitely before, I wouldn't advise anyone doing it while they sleep.

Another couple went to reception to complain, saying that, "We have booked a room with a view, but we're unhappy because the only view we can see is of the car park". There's just no pleasing some people.

There are loads of these to come folks so stay tuned.

Once all the guests had gone we were released and free to go and do as we please. I honestly don't think I liked any home port anywhere near as much as the one on my first contract. We were in Palma de Mallorca in Tenerife. This port was walking distance to the city centre, internet cafes, shopping mall, arcade and bowling alley. On top of all that it was just a ten-minute taxi to the beach, and 30 minute ride to the nearest water park, what more could you want?! Around the beach were many English themed pubs and bars which were always full of shirtless loud-mouth northerners covered in tribal tattoos, which was ...nice. The internet café was always full of crew who went to Skype home, and there was a fantastic bar next to it which served beer in frozen glasses, which on a hot day was absolute heaven. It was such a convenient port to be at once a week as there was always something to do or somewhere to go, whether it was a group meal, shopping trip or beach visit.

If you had been on the morning disembarkation shift you would have the rest of the day off until the sail away deck party that evening, and if you hadn't worked that morning then you would be working in the afternoon checking in the embarking guests. The majority of us preferred to be on the morning shift so that we could have the rest of the day free, but if you were on embarkation it meant you could have a lay in and catch up on your drinking the night before, so plenty of pros and cons there. If of course drinking wasn't your thing then you could get up and off early to go and get your bits done before your shift started. A lot of information there but as another cruise ship saying goes, 'Every night is Friday night, and every morning is Monday morning.'

A couple of times I went to bed thinking I wasn't getting up until the afternoon, but first thing in the morning I would be awoken by my cabin phone and be informed that I had to cover someone for disembark for whatever reason. Those were painful mornings as I didn't exactly have a chance to wake up properly. I would splash some water on my face, slap some gel in my hair and quickly brush my teeth before charging out my cabin and up to the quayside. From that point on I was running around frantically relaying and receiving messages through a walkie-talkie. I would be chasing after guests carrying their luggage because they had conveniently forgotten to pick it up at the gangway (or so they said nonchalantly), helping soon-to-be-deads and over-feds on to the coach, doing a final farewell speech and then sending them off to the airport. Oh, and on most of these types of mornings I would be hungover as hell and it would be raining cats and dogs.

As I said before, the upside to doing disembark was having the rest of the day to yourself, the downside was that the guests were generally a lot more impatient, uncooperative and inconsiderate. This is probably because they were having to face the reality that their holiday was at an end, and now they must return back to blighty for their nine-to-fives. In a direct contrast whenever guests would arrive at the ship, the majority would be in high spirits because their holiday was about to begin.

There was a healthy level of competition between the other ents hosts and I, and one such competition came at the end of every cruise when the guests would have the opportunity to fill out a CSQ (Customer Satisfaction Questionnaire). It was at the weekly team meetings when we would go through some of these to see who out of all of us had been mentioned by name the most in positive comments. For me it was just a bit of fun, but for others it was coal for the fire that stoked their egos (as I was not yet able to host events on the microphone, I didn't have an ego in much need of stoking). On the last night of the cruise I remember overhearing colleagues sometimes asking guests politely if they would be able to write about them in the comments as it would be helping them out and tip the odds in their favour. But the next morning, once the CSQs had all been filled out their attitude towards the guests was that of indifference. They had served their purpose and now it was out with the old, in with the new. *Yeah whatever cheers thanks bye.*

As soon as the new guests arrived the contest was back on to see who could win over the most guests for the next cruise. For a lot of people first impressions are long lasting, so a popular theory among some of my colleagues was that when the guests came to filling out the CSQs at the end, they would probably remember the first positive experience they had. For us hosts the very first chance we had to make an impression was the 'welcome to the ship' speech given on the coach. So when they arrived from the airport, my colleagues would battle for the chance to do the welcome speech as it was a chance to boost their profiles and get in early with the guests. There was a speech to follow but most of us just went off script and we did our own versions of it, throwing as much of ourselves into it as possible with the intent to make the guests laugh. To this day I still remember the speech word for word:

Embarkation speech

Hola! **(Pause for them to respond)**

*Oh, muy bien, buenas tardes,
bienvenido, cómo estás!?*

**(Pause for them to look a little
worried and to think they might
be in the wrong place)**

Don't worry folks, I am English.
(Laughter pause)

Welcome everyone to the **(ship's
name)**, *my name's* **(your name)**
*and I'm one of your entertainment
staff here on- board ... obviously.*
(Laughter pause)

*In a moment's time we'll get you
off the coach but first let me just
tell you what you gotta do next.
Firstly you'll all need to grab your
luggage, head inside the terminal
and have a welcome on-board
snap with our photographer. Then
come over and see my colleagues
and me where we will be handing
out envelopes which contain your
cabin keys. Once you've got these
move on up to the front desk at the
end of the terminal to see our*

*wonderful reception staff where they will give you some labels. You will need to attach these to all of your luggage so that it can be delivered to your cabin. Please allow up to one hour for us to do this before registering a formal complaint. **(Laughter pause)** Is anyone here all inclusive? **(Pause for them to respond)***

*Take a good look folks, this is the only time you're going to see these people sober. **(Laughter pause)***

*That's it from me folks now let's go have a great cruise! **(The crowd goes wild)**.*

Pretty good right? Ah well if you didn't laugh it's probably because I wrote down 'laughter pause' where people usually laughed. Canned laughter helps encourage audiences to enjoy themselves when it comes to stuff on TV, but it's harder to achieve with the written word. Like any speech it's all in the delivery, take it too seriously and run the risk of sounding like a headmaster addressing his pupils in full assembly, don't take it serious enough and lose the respect and attention of your audience completely. At the beginning of my first contract my welcome speech didn't start off as it was written above, I literally read it from the clipboard as it was written just trying to get the words out and not mess up. This was, after all, the first time I had ever been in front of an audience and spoken on a microphone which for me at the time was kind of a big deal. It felt like I was dipping my toes in at the shallow end and nervously going in deeper and deeper. Gradually, week by week I would gain more confidence and my trial and error system helped me evolve the speech into something that got the laughs every time.

There's a fine line to be drawn in having a little bit of fun and having too much. If whilst onstage it appears like you are having more fun than the audience, then that's when you need to dial it back, after all, you're there to entertain them and not the other way around. For me, tongue-in-cheek kind of humour usually went down well as the guests had been travelling all day, so I did my best to play up to my youth as I knew that was the way most of them perceived me anyway. I would play up to missing my parents which would strike an empathetic chord in the hearts of some of the guests, and as a by-product, I'd eventually start to get away with slightly cheekier remarks. That style seemed to be working for me but what works for one doesn't necessarily work for the other.

Now and then it got pretty competitive during dual hosted events, as my colleagues would try to outdo each other when it came to thinking up puns and put downs. Sometimes what started off as just a bit of fun, friendly, on-stage banter between them, would take a turn into passive aggressive behaviour. The remarks would begin to shift from playfully innocent teasing to snide personal attacks. As the intensity between the hosts brewed mid-show you could feel the atmosphere among the guests intensify, as the laughter gradually began to subside. Some comments made were just flat out disrespectful and you could actually hear guests gasp out of shock. As I sat and watched these events unfold from the side-lines (as I was still not able to host), I took note of how not to rise to this kind of hosting mentality. Trying to get one over on one of your co-hosts just creates unnecessary friction, and the entertainment is supposed to be suitable for a family audience. I'm not suggesting that we were supposed to be hosting events like a patronising episode of Rainbow, but it definitely shouldn't be conducted as if it were a rap battle from 8 Mile. I made a decision back then to deliberately avoid putting anyone down in front of an audience to make myself look better, although I'll admit it was partly due to the fact I was worried about retaliation, getting seriously burnt, freezing up with the mic at my lips and having a crowd of people chanting 'CHOKE' in my face … just like B-Rabbit.

My ACD Gary would have the audacity to rip on guests by likening them to people known in pop culture. Simpletons like The Dingles, for example. He got away with it because he had plenty of stage time to gain their trust and to build that kind of rapport so they roared with laughter. I thought I might try it and see what kind of response I'd get. To my surprise it didn't go down so well, apparently people don't like it when the youth of today infer that they are of a lesser intelligence in front of a roomful of strangers. I learnt my lesson there, so I changed tactic to fit in with my on-board persona. I adopted what I called my two for one strategy, where I would make at least two self-deprecating statements at my own expense, before turning on one of the guests to keep a level playing field, and usually only if they were interfering or being difficult.

During practically every single quiz you would be reading out a question, and a guest not partaking would shout out the answer because they were soooo funny (you can practically taste my sarcasm there), so they would then become my prime targets for some kind of whimsical put down, and of course in this instance I had the guests fully on my side. Normally I'd just say something like "Yeah, alright, mouth!" but inside what I would've really liked to have said was *Yeah, nice one, dickhead!*

I think the only time I ever received impassioned boos from an audience was when I attempted a re-telling of a joke I had heard from a colleague. It was during our on-board version of The Price is Right. Somewhere in the heart of the game I decided to go for it. "Ladies and Gentlemen it's such an honour to be hosting this show tonight, as I'm sure most of you have already probably heard the sad news today, that the much beloved Bruce Forsyth has sadly passed away." (This is back when he was still alive) In unison the audience let out a collective *"Awwww"*. I went on to say, "Can anyone tell me how old he actually was?" Then a range of mixed ages was called out to which I replied, "No, higher ... lower!" Cue the boooo and cut to me getting a bollocking from Gary later that night.

I remember around the middle of my first contract a new guy joined my team to replace someone. He was a fully competent host and had a lot of microphone experience with another company previously. He got huge belly laughs from the guests right from the start and it was going well for him. I should however point out that entertainers are known to be divas, and quite territorial. Gary called the new guy into his office one day to tell him that he was the funny guy on ship, and that he got the big laughs on-board for his raunchy brand of comedy. He then declared how he had been doing comedy for over twenty years, and told the new guy he wasn't allowed to do any of his material any–more. Whenever you got into semantics with Gary about whether something was funny or not, his response would always be, "let me tell you something, I've been doing this a long time and I know funny ... and I am funny!" Such modesty. He had a lot of whimsical quirks around the ship that made him quite an endearing character, his level of charisma was rather infectious and I actually learnt a quite a lot from him, in spite of him being a bit egocentric. The new guy didn't exactly adhere willingly to this entertainment dictator regime being forced upon him, and so he carried on as normal. After only two weeks of being on-board he was fired for having sex with a passenger in a lifeboat. I was sad to see him go but it wouldn't be the last time we would cross paths.

You might be thinking to yourself, *But Sam! You're funny and stuff, why didn't Gary ever give you the talk about not stealing his thunder?* I guess because I hadn't really found my comedy voice at this time. To be honest I'm still trying to find it. I was a hot mess deer in headlights the guests laughed *at* rather than *with*, and during game shows, I would often play the bit part of fall guy, to make whoever was hosting seem to be a bully and worthy of booing (in a fun way). Some game shows I would pretend to have been mugged by a passenger and would come on from side stage with my clothes ruffled and my hair all dishevelled in order to elicit sympathy.

Looking back I know that this was a rather demeaning role, but honestly I was okay with it because I was making people happy and glad to be of service, even if I was serving by playing a character who was, on the surface, oblivious. Well ... that's my story and I'm sticking to it!

During a typical embarkation most of the time our well-trained British guests would form orderly queues and wait their turn, but add VIPS, disabled passengers, guest acts, returning crew and anyone impatient into the mix, then the whole thing became a fiasco. People would bypass the queue and rudely interrupt others whilst they were being served. We'd get complaints from people before they had even gotten on-board because we had failed to provide them with a four-poster bed, spa treatment, steak dinner and free booze during their two-hour flight from the UK ...

Because the airline was the same company as the cruise line we were all made to feel responsible for any and all problems that occurred during a customer's entire experience. It didn't seem to occur to them that we had nothing to do with any of the operations that took place prior to their arrival at the ship. Still, when it comes to the question, 'who do I complain to?' a nametag with a company logo by default always makes you a prime target. Such classic complaints included:

Guest: "The air conditioning on the coach wouldn't reach my face, the seat belt next to me was broken, the windows were dirty, I didn't have my glasses so I couldn't see out the window, there were too many stray animals that were far too skinny and the arm rest on my seat was uncomfortable!"

My favourite complaint concerning the terminal itself was:

Guest: "I thought the ship would be a lot bigger. Why is it so small!? This isn't what was advertised in the brochure or what I've paid for!"
Response: "Madam, this is the quayside terminal, the ship is just behind us."

In addition to the complaints we got a lot of stupid, *stupid* questions. I say stupid twice because some of them were just that stupid. These examples should give you some idea of what I'm talking about:

Guest: "Would it be possible to take a picture of the ship as it's leaving the port?" (Bit of a tricky one that).
Response: "Yes of course, if you would just like to hang back a while, wait till everyone has boarded and the ship has set sail, I'm sure that can be arranged."

Guest: "Does the ship generate its own power?"
Response: "No, actually we run off an extension cable that we plug in at mainland."

Guest: "Why don't the inside cabins have a porthole?"

Guest: "Have I booked an outside or an inside cabin? I don't fancy an outside one, I imagine it will get too cold at night."

Guest: "Do you have to leave the ship to go on a shore excursion?"

Guest: "Do you allow water skiing off the back of the boat?"

Guest: "What do you do with the ice carvings after they melt?"

Guest: "Is the island completely surrounded by water?"

Honestly folks, you can't write this stuff, people actually ask these questions and a lot more regularly than you would think. Don't worry though, there will be more of these to come. I did struggle with how I should implement these ridiculous questions into this book, but rather than try to carve out a unique story for each one, I figured I have enough of my own material to get through without going on a load of other people's tangents. You're too busy, I'm too busy, we're all too busy! So thanks again if you're reading this book.

Even though I could in theory spend a lot of time complaining about the long hours on-board, the seven day working week and the fast-paced environment that hardly even seemed to let up, I think it would be far more interesting to tell you all how I managed to keep a firm hold of my sanity during the most intense customer service based period of my life. Back in the terminal my colleagues and I would be dealing with all kinds of problems. Quite commonly you would get the odd bigot who would ask a receptionist, "Do you speak English?" and with a Russian lilt they would usually reply, "Yes, I speak English very good." This is a perfectly acceptable answer (even though spell checker just tried to get me to change the word 'good' for 'well') but to the average bigot, it's just not good enough and they become instantly enraged. "NO! I want someone English! Why is everyone here from another f@%*ing country?" Unfortunately with over 1000 new people coming on-board each week, the odds are that there's at least one of these guests every cruise.

As Mary Poppins once famously said, "In every job that must be done there is an element of fun, you find the fun aaaand snap! The job's a game!" I kind of took this advice on-board (as in on a personal level not as a carry on). I have pretty much lived by this philosophy for most of my life. Obviously we all have rules, regulations, codes of conduct and health and safety to protect ourselves, but what's life without living a little dangerously from time to time? There is always a way to turn the most mundane of tasks into something more stimulating even if ever so slightly. Whether it be for all to join in with, or just something for you internally. For example when the guests approach you in the terminal they state their name and you hand them their envelope which contains their room key. In my mind, before they had spoken, I was trying to pair their face to a name on the table based purely on their appearance. Sometimes I'd get it right and excitedly make a point of letting them know that. "Ahh I knew you looked like a John Humphreys!" to which they would respond with a look of confusion and say, "Errr … okay?" On one occasion however my past caught up with me and one of the guests said, "I recognise you from somewhere. Yeah … didn't you used to push the trolleys around Asda car park?" which of course I had done, but not to my colleagues' knowledge. For whatever reason I'd kept it a secret from them so at the time I found this particular recognition to be rather embarrassing.

I literally just remembered another game I used to play with my family and it's worth sharing I think. If you ever watched the TV show Embarrassing Bodies then you might have already played it. Basically the patient is telling the doctor what is wrong with them but usually the symptoms are quite vague and ambiguous. So when the Doctor says, "Okay, let's take a look shall we?" that's when you pause it and everyone has a guess at what they think the problem might be. No one wins, we're all just a bunch of massive losers.

Usually, just as we were awaiting the arrival of the last coach of the day, we would get a message through from management via walkie-talkie telling us that the flight had been delayed. Suddenly all dreams of having any time to yourself that day would quickly up and vanish. The flight delay was a how-long-is-a-piece-of-string conundrum, as it would mean we would be stranded in the terminal until all the guests arrived, and it would potentially mean a later departure time from the port. It was during this time that we would be able to feel our brains corroding unless we did something about it, and do something about it we did, as the only real benefit to being stuck in this situation was the general lack of authority. When you are working on-board you are under constant scrutiny and supervision from superior staff and officers. However in the terminal these personnel were either busy on-board or off duty ashore having the time of their lives ... probably. So at this time, the terminal offered a slice of freedom from work whilst at work. In a way, the terminal could be a fair representation of Limbo, as it lies directly between the ship (which is Hell) and in this case, Palma de Mallorca (Heaven).

So in the absence of authority my colleagues and I would be trapped but also free, and it wasn't long before we were playing games and messing about with anything we could get our hands on. All the envelopes that we had already handed out to the guests earlier had been wrapped securely into bundles with elastic bands. We kept a box under the table to discard them in and by day's end we had amassed ourselves quite a collection. We'd divvy them out equally and soon be diving around the terminal firing them at each other, ducking for cover and skidding about in our socks on the highly polished laminate flooring. This all sounds incredibly childish, but how often do you as an adult get the opportunity to partake in full on play warfare? The options are open to you, laser tag, paintball, shooting ranges etc. but the answer to the question remains the same, how often do <u>you</u> get to do this?

Answer: Not enough!

Then there were the epic office chair races. Using cones, queuing posts and boxes, a hodgepodge racetrack would be collaboratively created. Then it was voted that the absolutely stunning receptionist from Mauritius would be our flag girl. She looked a bit like a teenier version of Lucy Liu, and when she wasn't working we would use little Archie from the Philippines who made a fantastic comedic substitute. The race would often get out of hand rather quickly, with dirty tactics, sabotage and violence being used like a live action episode of wacky races.

This evolved into another game whereby the winner of the race would get the chance to punish the loser. Punishments came in a variety of forms. Sometimes it was trying to knock a plastic cup off their head by firing elastic bands at them (but obviously not without a few deliberately failed attempts first). Another punishment was that the victor got to use the loser as their own personal bowling ball. This was achieved by making the loser sit in an office chair and have them hold on to a plastic linked chain. Then the winner (holding the other end of the chain) would swing them around in circles across the floor like a hammer throw and release them into a set of traffic cones that had been pre-arranged into a triangle. As is typical, just as whoever was careening towards a potential strike the delayed coach would be pulling up alongside the terminal to see the display. Amazingly and thankfully no one ever complained ... or got hurt.

Once the very last envelope in the tray was handed out, that was it, done, finished, thank god! Almost immediately after we would all look at our watches to see if there was enough time. Hardly ever did we like to admit to ourselves that there wasn't enough time, and we would often kid ourselves that we did, even if technically we didn't, but ultimately we never deprived ourselves of what it was we so desperately sought. And that, my friends, was a carafe of vino or a couple bottles of cerveza at a little establishment in town called Mr Smiles. God I used to love that place, not just for the name but for what it represented. The sheer fact that we had just managed to do a complete turnover of guests was such a massive sigh of relief every time. The idea of going straight back to the ship afterwards was the last thing any of us wanted, as we all knew deep down we would have to deal with them imminently with the sail away deck party. So we would synchronise watches and say, "Right, back here in five minutes!" then race off back to our rooms to get changed out of our stifling work clothes and into something a bit more comfortable, dash back to the meeting point, and then charge over to Mr Smiles for a well-earned drink.

When we were finally able to clink glasses at those rare moments that signified the end of one long week and the start of the next, we would all feel a shared sense of accomplishment. Mr Smiles genuinely was one of the few bars that really stands out for me, as it was there for me like a shoulder to cry on, a friend to laugh with, or a motherly cuddle to let me know everything was going to be all right. It didn't matter that none of the staff there spoke any English (after all why would they? We were in Spain) but as a team we were confident enough to collectively speak the basics, such as beer, wine, please, thank you and the bill. However on one occasion I was starving, and there was just enough time to get something to eat. Sometimes we get a craving for something and no matter how good the options on the menu look, our mind is made up and the heart just wants what the heart wants. For me it was a fried egg sandwich and nothing else. I thought this was easily something anyone could whip up even if it wasn't on the menu so

I asked the waiter for one. "Que?" he replied. I went blank for a moment, and realised that I knew hardly any Spanish to help me with my request. The only word that came close by affiliation was pollo which means chicken and that's not what I wanted. So what did I do? I performed my request in the form of a charade. I started by pointing at myself and announcing to the table, "I ... Pollo", then moving on to a bit of light clucking and wing flapping just to prove I was serious. Then I proceeded to squat down nice and low, strain and produce an imaginary egg which I held above my head proudly with a look of delight. I then got out my pretend non-stick frying pan and cracked in an egg. I made a sizzling sound effect and efficiently lifted it out and plonked it between two slices of imaginary bread. The waiter to my absolute joy got it in one. *"AH! Si si, senor, muy bien."*

When mime is all you have left it helps if you do it properly, and I'm not ashamed to admit that I count this story as one of my favourite personal triumphs. That might well make you think that if the bar is set this low, then the rest of my stories must be pretty pants. I remind you that this book is for the everyman, and is not set in a fantasy world where I play the hero, slay magical beasts and save a damsel in distress. Nor does this book go on highly improbable tangents, whereby I go on to defend the guests against a group of a tyrannical pirates who are out to steal our booty. The stories I tell are far more relatable (I hope) and even though most of them have no real point, life lesson or moral outcome, I wouldn't be doing my job as an entertainer if I didn't try to make you laugh. This is not the Hero's journey, this is the fool's trundle.

Now I've already said a bit about the sail away deck party so I won't go on about it again, but seriously, this is a great way to spend the first moments of a cruise and is usually the perfect end to a long day for everyone. However, the following day would be our day at sea. This is when the ship spends all day out on the ocean waves sailing to its next destination hence the name … day at sea. In terms of my workload this was the day I worked the hardest as the entertainment was back to back all day long. I would like to say that I enjoyed these days because there was so much to see and do on-board, but every week it would be pretty much the same thing, and it wouldn't take too long for me to get tired of the routine and become an expert power napper.

First thing in the morning would be the passenger safety drill, Hooray! Normally ships are required to do a safety drill for the guests on the same day they arrive, but seeing as our guests would not all be on-board until the evening, it was by that time too late to have one. So the next best thing was to have it first thing in the morning which all the guests absolutely loved obviously!

When I think about safety drills in general, I vividly remember being fast asleep back in my cabin, and then being instantly awoken from my slumber by the ship's loud alarm bells followed by an officer's voice announcing the commencement of the drill. Nothing quite like being eased gently into the day is there? Typically after this announcement you could hear a collective unified groan that would echo throughout the crew corridors, but we all got up and out of bed anyway, as we knew we were all in the same boat ∴ literally.

I'm not a morning person by any means, and I am definitely not a morning person when my day starts this way. My usual routine on these mornings was to roll out of bed onto the floor, where my clothes would conveniently already be waiting. Then I would slither into them like a snake sheds its skin but in reverse. Once half decent I'd crawl into my bathroom, and have some fun slapping myself around until I began to feel some feeling in my face. My morning beauty regime was an integral part of the day, as I would usually spend a whole minute if not less getting ready. After I'd finished brushing my teeth I'd scoop a blob of something hair product related onto my centre parting, then smoosh it around a bit before covering it with my favourite funky bright orange safety drill cap. Then I'd grab my matching orange life jacket, pop it over my head and leave the cabin yawning and stretching (what a professional). Just as soon as I had woken, I found myself embedded among human traffic which was wall to wall. Both crew and guests making their way to the drill with the enthusiasm of a funeral march, but once they were all out on the open deck and able to breathe the clean sea air, most of them would perk right up.

The basic idea behind this drill is so the guests know how to get to their designated lifeboat (or muster stations) in the case of an emergency.

In their lifejackets standing shoulder to shoulder, the guests would line up in a nice neat grid on deck, or at least that was the aim. Whilst everyone was getting into position the cruise director made the all-important safety announcement that I have burned into my memory on account of having heard it so many times.

Now as luck would have it, my position on-board as an entertainer actually gave me some seniority when it came to passenger drills, and it wasn't long before I was given a manageable amount of responsibility, when I was informed that I would be undertaking the prestigious role of muster station leader. This is the person who at your muster station will call out the register to make sure all are accounted for. I didn't go power mad or let the title go to my head, I stayed professional and performed my duties to the best of my ability ... for about five minutes. I couldn't help it! I had an audience right in front of me and simply couldn't resist the opportunity to perform. Part of my routine was miming along with cruise director Stewart's announcement. When it came to showing the guests how to don their life jackets, just like flight attendants before take-off, I would do my best to ham it up so much that my guests would all be chuckling along, and guests at other stations would start peering over and secretly wish they could be in the fun lifeboat...   probably.

I had a few jokes that over time I picked up from my colleagues that made the drill a bit more fun, such as: "Ladies and gents there is now going to be a demonstration on how to safely jump from the ship … can I borrow someone's child please?" occasionally I did receive a few over eager parents pushing their children forwards.

Another bit I used to roll out was, "Okay so here's how it's going to work folks, it's women and children first, exactly like the Titanic. The reason they go in first is because they get seated all around the outside of the boat, then the men go in afterwards and use the women and children as a windbreaker, and as an added bonus, if the engine fails, guess who's rowing?"

The laughter from the guests did unfortunately attract the unwanted attention of senior officers who somehow got the impression that I wasn't taking the drill as seriously as it was intended. It was after a stern talking to in the staff captain's office one day, that I altered my conduct to meet with the officers' expectations. However, a few weeks later I was just standing in front of my guests feeling a little awkward and a little bored, so I casually asked, "is anyone going on any nice shore excursions today?" (which of course they wouldn't be, because we were at sea). The guests' laughter resulted in me getting relieved of my muster station leader status, and I was demoted to the rather demeaning role of lifeboat number sign holder.

There were actually a few joke announcements that got made by the cruise director. Specifically on April Fool's Day when we advertised that passengers could try their hand at deep sea fishing, and visit the ship's glass bottom so they could take pictures of underwater activity. As you would expect, there were a few gullible guests who went down to the shore excursion desk, queued up and tried to book the tour and weren't best pleased when they were told that the tour did not exist, and essentially had the crushing realisation that they were in fact an idiot for believing such malarkey. This is of course hard medicine to swallow so those guests took one side step across to the reception desk to register a formal complaint, which is just typical really.

On sea days the reception area was where I used to start my ship tours from as it was a fairly central location on-board and relatively easy to get to. As with most of my duties they would be advertised in the on-board publication that went into every guest cabin called the Cruise News. A brief description of any activity or event, the location and starting time would be written inside. As staff we are expected to be in the practice of arriving to each duty fifteen minutes early to either set up or to be there to intercept any over eager participants. If no one showed up then obviously we couldn't just leave, we would have to wait for fifteen minutes past the starting time in case people were late. In the example of the ship tours I would quite often be hurried by the guests who had turned up early to leave closer to the start time because they didn't feel they should have to wait for those who were running late. So, I would have to take them on their tour which ends back at reception, only to find a group of angry guests sat there waiting for me, so I'd have to do it again wouldn't I!

I'd have those rare cruises where everyone on-board was of the shared mentality that they could find their bearings all by themselves, but most weeks I'd get a gaggle of guests who required someone to show them how to navigate the ship. I'm not saying that those people were simple, I would never insinuate that, no not me, never! When you first board the ship and begin walking around it can sometimes be quite overwhelming. So a guided tour of all the ship's points of interest sounds quite reassuring to some I'm sure. For others, they might come expecting a bit more information other than just, *this is the restaurant, this is the salon, and this is the showroom* etc. But on some of the ships I worked, that sort of information was all we had been scripted to basically say. It was only after a few months of doing ship tours that I began to accrue additional knowledge from the guests themselves like the ship's history, where and when it was built, what its gross tonnage, weight, length and height were. The internet wasn't as readily available to me back then as it is now, so whenever I got the chance to get online and check in with my friends and family, researching the ship I worked on 24/7 was the last thing I ever wanted to do.

In terms of making my so-called mark, as in the title of this chapter, who's to say if I did or didn't make one of any sizeable impact. My guess is that I probably didn't, because at this early stage at the beginning of my first contract; I was mostly just along for the ride, but more than happy to be so.

Chapter 4

There Are No Stupid Questions … Hah!

I've just decided that I'm now too far into this book to keep flinging these silly guest stories at you intermittently.

I'm dedicating a chapter to all that is foolish, as I'm determined to finish up with these stories and move on once and for all. This way, we no longer have to endure questions that make our brains hurt. It might be entertaining but I feel partly responsible for destroying valuable brain cells.

*Disclaimer! Unfortunately, these stories are all true and are a mixture of things I personally encountered and things I collected from colleagues over the years. Hold on to your sanity.

Guest: "Do the crew get to eat the passengers' leftovers for their meals?"

To which I usually replied, "Oh no, the company saves money on feeding the crew <u>actual</u> food, by providing us all with our meals in pill supplement form."

Amazingly I did get this question a number of times, and usually the guest's response was a hearty chuckle, but once or twice I recall the guest's agape jaw and a look of utter shock.

Guest: "Do the crew live on-board?"

Now just where am I supposed to start with this one? OF COURSE THE BLOODY CREW LIVE ON THE BLOODY SHIP! What could someone possibly consider a legitimate alternative answer?! I'm pretty sure I can think up a number of ludicrous responses that would be a clear attempt at sarcasm, like, "Oh the crew actually have their own underwater sea village rather similar to Atlantis. It's located beneath the ship and we tow it everywhere we go. It's great! We don't have to pay rent but we do have to pay for our own oxygen and dry cleaning." My best attempt at a serious reply, that <u>could</u> be considered plausible yet highly unlikely would be, "Actually the crew stay in company provided lodgings back on land. Every morning before the guests wake up and every night after they've all gone to bed, the crew are helicoptered on and off the ship." Where is the logic in this kind of operation? Of the few guests who asked me this question, one of them (and this is 100% true) at the end of their cruise genuinely wrote down in the CSQ form comments: "I had a most enjoyable cruise, however unfortunately, I was kept awake most nights due to the sound of the crew transport helicopters." Some mothers really do have 'em.

For a guest to bring me the cruise news and ask questions about a certain activity was a daily thing. No wait, make that bi-hourly thing, that's more accurate. One of my favourites was, "It says here that this activity takes place on Deck Five Forward, but which is Deck Five? And what does forward mean!?" Now whether you choose to take me at my word is up to you, but believe it or not, Deck Five is the fifth deck on-board, but for some reason, guests confused floors and decks to mean two entirely different things completely. You can't walk very far in any direction without seeing a sign somewhere informing you of what deck you are on, and if you still haven't found a sign, then there is no shortage of crew on hand for you to ask either. A helpful tip to remember what 'forward' means is that it is at the forward of the ship, rather than at the back. Not logical enough? Try looking out of the window and see which way the water is going and work it out from there.

It's so hard not to sound passive aggressive whilst writing this chapter. If I ever do an audio book version then I'll be sure I'm calm and relaxed before tackling this section.

There are a few nautical terms which can easily confuse non-seafaring folk, such as bow, aft, stern, port and starboard. So to briefly explain as best I can, the bow is the same as forward and is the pointy bit at the front of the ship. Its pronounced bow as in bow before your king, not bow as in bow-tie. Although to think of a bow-tie is also a helpful way to remember that it means at the top/front/forward/head.

Stern and aft mean the same thing and depending on your accent, aft is pronounced similarly to how you would say either ass or arse, so keeping that in mind is helpful to remembering that aft is at the back end of the ship. It is not short for shaft, raft or daft.

Finally port and starboard are always getting mixed up. They just mean left and right so long as you are facing forward. The only thing you need to remember is which one is which, and there is an old mnemonic that goes: 'There is no port **left** in the glass'. So there you go, port is left. I just googled phrases for remembering which way is starboard, but I don't think anyone else has really bothered to coin one. It seems that the collective maritime community has all just shrugged their shoulders and gone, *Ahh we've done one mnemonic, why do we have to bother with another one? Surely they can work out what the other one is by process of elimination?!* and they would be **right** not to bother with a phrase for starboard … wouldn't they ;)

Sometimes people love to complain just for the sake of complaining … I *don't like this ship, you have to walk so far to get to everything.* If you have ongoing physical pain and great difficulty walking then I totally understand and sympathise with the complaint, however if you don't then you're probably one of the types of people who would most likely love to have their own electric seat to take them all over the ship at the push of a button, like the ones on-board the futuristic space ship in Disney/Pixar's 2008 film WALL·E, you know? For all them fat bastards.

Believe it or not some people are considered to be professional complainers, mainly because they do it full time. Their aim is to try and squeeze as much free stuff out of people as possible, in order to feel better about themselves because they were able to work a system to their advantage. Of course it doesn't always work, but you have to admire some of them for trying. *I've been playing Bingo all week and didn't win a single game! I want a refund for the cost of my tickets!* Who says these things?! Bingo is gambling! You wouldn't complain to a casino manager that a one-armed bandit is stealing your money, unless of course you had literally just been robbed by a bandit with one arm.

Some guests are simply unable to grasp the most basic of concepts, like for example the physical disintegration of a building over time is a natural process called erosion. Freestanding buildings outdoors up against the elements for centuries tend to erode and decay organically. One afternoon I asked a guest if they enjoyed their time out in Rome, and they slapped me in the face hard with a triple dose of stupidity:

Guest: "Yeah I went to the sixteen (Sistine) chapel but to be honest I didn't really enjoy it, there were far too many Italians about, and I don't know why those romans went and built so many bloody ruins."

On more than one occasion I was asked by a guest to show them where the pool table was. I pulled myself together, and calmly spoke the following words which were difficult to utter without any hinted tone of condescension, "I'm sorry, but we do not have a pool table on-board." The guest would then extend the query. "Why not? Surely you must have one!" It's then that I would have to bite my lip and grind my teeth (internally of course) and peacefully explain, "We don't have one … because it wouldn't work." I'd give them a few seconds for the penny to drop, and if it looked like it was causing them some serious inner pain I would compose myself and add, "Think about it … spherical shapes … on a flat table … on a moving ship?" and as the look of realisation slowly crept over their furrowed brows, they would nod their head in acknowledgment and say, "Ahh yes, I'm with you, I'm with you." Then they'd come out with the clanger: "So why don't you just nail the legs to the floor then?" *Sigh*.

I once heard tale of an elderly woman in her mid-80's who was vacationing alone on her very first cruise. From her cabin she called reception and asked the receptionist how to get out of her cabin. That's right, you read that correctly. The receptionist, initially stunned by the question, proceeded to give careful instruction on how one would navigate one's own way out of one's own cabin ... as one does. "Okay my dear, so you just need to open the front door and that will lead you out into the corridor, okay?" And the precious old dear came right back with one of the sweetest, most innocent sentences I have ever heard. "Ah yes, but there are two doors in my cabin. One leads into the toilet and the other door says please do not disturb!" The receptionist informed me that they did not see that old lady for the rest of the cruise. Poor woman was too considerate for her own good.

A room stewardess confided in me that one time a guest called them over and asked if they could possibly fix their cabin microwave for them. Before the stewardess could tell them that cabins were not equipped with microwaves, the guest ushered them in and pointed directly at a securely locked safe. The confusion was an honest one, and to be fair the guest must have mistaken it for a microwave because safes, in many ways are very much like a microwaves. They are rectangular, they are metal, they have numbered keypads and they both have instructions on front of them explaining how to operate a safe ... don't they? Or is that, oh no wait, that's just safes. I love how the sudden realisation of something that was so obvious must have whacked the guest over the head, and made them blurt out the first thought that came to mind. "What's the combination for the safe?" the guest asked. "If I knew that," said the stewardess, "the safe wouldn't be as safe would it now?"

Most evenings (especially on formal night) you can hardly walk a few paces in guest areas without being requested to take pictures of everyone in all their finery. I quickly became quite adept at operating cameras, and was soon a self-taught self-proclaiming expert. I was competent enough to make it look as though I had been taking pictures since I was old enough to dribble. I would get so into it I was calling out poses, popping in and out of squats, lunging, reclining and dancing all around them like an excitable woodland sprite. Whenever a guest handed me their expensive hi-tech camera with an overwhelming amount of buttons and functions, most of the time they would clock that look in my eyes that would confidently suggest I could handle it, and so they would re-join their group without feeling the need to offer me any operational instruction, and so I was able to bathe for a brief moment in the knowledge that I, Sam Catling, was a competent, intelligent and trustworthy adult. Until an OAP interrupts my metaphorical bath and asks me to take their picture, hands me their stone-age brick of a camera, points to the stand alone singular bright red button staring me in the face, and carefully explains that in order to take their picture, I would have to aim the camera in their direction and next I would have to *just press the red button, that one just there.*

I once made the schoolboy error of asking an elder to take a snap of my colleagues and me, and failing to remember that instruction was most probably needed, the octogenarian held the camera up to their face the wrong way round, pressed their finger on the zoom in button, poked themselves square in the eye with the fully extended lens, dropped my camera on to the unforgiving pavement and managed to accidentally take a creepy looking picture of their eyeball up close.

We had a photography team on-board, and it was their job to capture every conceivable Kodak moment for the guests during their cruise. On the last day of the cruise all the pictures would be out on display so you could riffle through the vast selection and purchase the ones you liked.

"How do we tell which photos ours are?" I overheard a guest ask. "You'll be in them" was the photographer's sage advice. "Oh yeah!" they laughed nervously. "And what do you do with the ones that you don't sell?" No one likes to think that leftover food in a restaurant goes to waste, so why should leftover photos be any different? The idea of a room with multiple shredders hard at work, turning happy holidaymakers' memories into rabbit hutch bedding is an unsettling thought, especially as rabbits aren't allowed on-board and also because ingesting too much photo ink is poisonous and they could die! What would the guests like us to do with the unsold pictures of them? Hold on to them in case they ever come back and decide that actually they would like to buy their pictures from their cruise back in 2008. Would they like to think that perhaps the unsold photographs could act as a backup to the voyage data recorder (which is the cruise ship equivalent to a black box on commercial airplanes)? Do they think that a collection of the unsold pictures is being gathered so we can make a time capsule for future generations to see? That way we can show them just how much fun they had posing against the many various backdrops on offer, and how quickly they were able to gain weight during their short stay on-board. Or do they think we decorate our cabins with them because we miss them all so much? Incidentally, a young lad who was a repeat cruiser came back and told me how the picture he had taken with me on his first cruise, now sat perched on-top of his bedside nightstand back home, which I found to be both sweet and a little bit creepy as to be honest as we'd hardly even spoken.

I can't speak for what the photography department on every ship do with unsold photographs, my educated guess would be that they destroy them all, and with a sadistic amount of pleasure. That's probably a very accurate assumption, however some of the photographers on one of the ships I worked would scour the rejects for the very best pictures to add to their scrapbook, which they had unfortunately titled … Minger of the Week. I'm sure I don't need to go into detail about the kind of pictures that made up the content of said scrapbook, but if you are unfamiliar with the term 'minger' then just understand that the photos were all of the highly unflattering variety. If you are thinking what monsters these individuals are for compiling such a cruel collage of cringe, please just try to understand, their job was incredibly boring most of the time, and they were just doing whatever they could to pass the time, so who could blame them?

I'd often get people who asked questions that they had clearly given some thought to, and when I say given thought to, I mean that they thought they would try to ask something that sounded clever and not so absurd that they would come across as a bit dim, but only a tiny fragment of thought actually went into the question itself, and the outcome would result in them asking a question that was rather absurd and made them come across a bit dim.

Guest: "How high are we above sea level?"

You can't really write these kind of questions can you? All I can do is write around it and try to expose it for what it is. This person might have thought it was a clever question because it's not every day they get to ask a question like it, but why this person thought to ask how high above sea level we were whilst we were at sea level is beyond me. That's like asking for the price of an individual item inside a 99p store. It feels awkward when you have to answer someone's question when they had already answered it in the asking. "Hmmm, by my calculations, we're not that high off sea level as we are currently at sea level, so if you've a fear of heights then please do not worry".

Sticking with the theme of the sea ...

Guest: "Is the water in the toilet seawater?"

Why the guest needed to know this I will never fully understand. I'd imagine that if it was pure sea water, then it would have probably left a layer of salt around the rim of the bowl like a margarita, but if you're not satisfied with the answer 'probably' and you're curious enough to investigate personally, taste it and find out.

On a serious note though, all the ship's water more or less does come from the sea, however, the purification process is a complicated engineering miracle, and far too difficult for me to explain. In layman's terms there's a bit of condensing and evaporating going on, an air brine educator and demister at work, and a vacuum gauge and vent cock also pulling their weight. This system desalinates sea water, and pumps fresh water around the ship for human consumption, toilets, sinks, showers and stuff. So hopefully that puts your mind at ease.

Guest: "Is the water in the pool seawater?"

This isn't actually that silly a question, but wait, give it a sec. I replied, "Yes, it is saltwater" and they said, "Oh I thought so ... because of the waves," for as we all know, water is always sea water so long as it's moving.

Moving on, we then have the people who feel cheated out of the chance to complain, because they have nothing to complain about. Like in the case of one couple, who went up to the reception desk at the end of their cruise and said, "We just wanted to say that we've both had such an amazing time, it's been incredible. I mean we really couldn't fault a single thing. Having said that we actually spent more on gratuities then we initially budgeted for, so we would like to be refunded please."

That seems fair enough right? I mean they've only done a nice thing with the intention of claiming a nice thing back, which is basically how the mafia operate. When told that they couldn't be refunded they immediately changed their tune and complained with genuine conviction.

Another guest took their redundant complaint straight to the very top. They cut through all the nonsense of dealing with middlemen, and went up to the captain to show him their recently filled sick bags as proof they weren't having the best of times. They blamed him for their dicky tummies personally, and requested that he post to their cabin a schedule of cruise itineraries in which they wouldn't get seasick. Some people simply don't get along with the high seas and motion sickness just gets to be too much for them. Personally I have no problem with the sway and swell of the ship, and actually find it rather comforting, especially at night when you're lying in bed and gently being rocked to sleep from side to side. Unless of course your bed faces in the wrong direction, then you end up hating it because as you lie there you end up feeling like a pointless human see-saw.

When the ship was rocking quite heavily, it's tough to figure out if everyone is having difficulty walking properly, or if they are all just pissed. When you spend a whole week on-board without getting off you get what is referred to as land sickness. This happens on planes as well but it's far more noticeable after extended periods at sea. Just as you were starting to get your sea legs you go ashore and forget how to use your land legs. Typical!

I never got seasick and thoroughly enjoyed it when we were swelling and swaying all over the place. When it got really bad the bar staff would wrap the whole bar end to end in cling film to prevent bottles falling off the counter. Waiters would frequently serve the guests their dinner in their lap, and housekeeping would very kindly leave sick bags tucked neatly inside the banisters on all the staircases. Isn't that thoughtful of them?

I remember one epic stormy night, as the wind whipped and whistled, we were having a crew party up on deck. Some of the team and I were running around like a bunch of idiots jumping in the air and trying to run to the front of the ship as it tilted backwards. Sort of like the uphill travellator at the end of Gladiators. When the ship leaned forwards the bow crashed down hard and sent a blast of water up in the air before hammering down on top of us. It was one of the most exhilarating experiences of my life, as the adrenaline was greater than any roller coaster I've ever been on. It even topped skydiving. I was as excited as Lieutenant Dan in Forest Gump in the shrimp boat storm scene. If you'd have given me an umbrella, I would have faded into obscurity and done a Mary Poppins for sure.

When the captain made an announcement telling us to get inside and stay there, we sulkily made our way inside kicking our heels as we went. I brushed off what felt like the equivalent of a saltshaker's worth of sea-salt off my face, and was met by a young boy crying hysterically. The violent sound of the waves clattering against the ship's hull was probably the culprit. He could only have been about five or six and he'd lost his mummy, bless him. So I did the only thing I could do in that situation, calm him down and take him to reception so we could put a call out for his mum to come collect him. The receptionist was extremely helpful as she instantly reassured the crying child that she had been on ships for three years now, and this was the first time that she was genuinely scared. The boy pondered this new information for just a second before the floodgates reopened with immediate effect. It was at that point I made myself scarce.

If you are one of the unlucky ones who is prone to sea sickness then there are a number of coping strategies and prevention techniques that some find useful. I've seen a lot of guests wearing Acupressure wristbands, which are basically just wristbands that have a little plastic ball stitched into them. The ball is supposed to rest on the veins of your wrists, gently pressing down onto a pressure point that is believed by practitioners of acupuncture to prevent nausea and vomiting. There's the argument that sea sickness is all in the mind so there are ways to trick it. For example if you're sitting inside and the ship and is swaying violently, then you could see the ship's handrail against the backdrop of the sea one second, and then up past the horizon and into the sky the next. This sends a message to the brain that the ship is out of control and brings on the feeling of motion sickness rather promptly. The solution? Stand directly behind the handrail and focus on the horizon. To the eye, the horizon won't look like its moving up and down as much as it was, so you can trick your mind into thinking that everything's smooth sailing.

Then come the old wives' tales on combating sea sickness, which include drinking ginger ale and eating biscuits, sliced apple, pumpkin seeds, and sitting on brown paper! (Who comes up with this shit?!). Of course you can also try over the counter remedies such as Kwells or Meclizine. Prescribed medication can be obtained for those of you who are utterly hopeless at sea. For severe cases, Scopolamine is often effective, and Compazine (Prochlorperazine) is traditionally injected directly into the ass meat. Both have been known to display some side effects such as constipation, blurred vision, dry mouth, drowsiness and dizziness. So to be on the safe side (and to cover my back) always consult with your GP before cruising so that you can kick the queasy nice and easy.

For the most part, the worst cases of seasickness occur on lifeboats, specifically when they are used to tender the guests to the port. This is when the ship has to anchor offshore as it's probably too big to be secured to the harbour, so the guests and crew are ferried back and forth. As the lifeboats are so small in comparison to the ship, you really feel the motion of the ocean once you encounter a bit of chop. You can literally see the colour of people's faces change just like a chameleon. When the seas were a bit on the rough side getting the guests in and out of the boats proved to be quite a challenge. As the boat was bobbing alongside the ship, people would slip, trip and fall, yell, push and shove, scream, cry and wail. It was quite dangerous sometimes, especially with the guests in wheelchairs and the handicapped, but amazingly I never heard of a really bad incident ever occurring.

The crew who were there to assist everyone were usually there all day long and did an amazing job every time. Unfortunately they were never really given the credit they deserved as the guests were all so preoccupied with their own health and safety. You could see in their facial expressions that they were making mental notes on how much of an inconvenience the whole ordeal had become, completely failing to remember that the weather is not something within our control.

I remember when we were in Zanzibar we had to tender to get ashore, but when the guests came to the jetty to be taken back to the ship, the tide had completely gone out and they were stranded for quite some time. I couldn't help but think that the locals had put that jetty there on purpose, because surely its placement would mean that this kind of problem would occur all the time, and that way they could prolong the guests' visit and milk them for every last penny.

On one particular excursion, we had tendered into port and gotten a minibus which went up the top of a cliff ridge and offered spectacular views. A concerned guest then asked, "How's the tender boat supposed to get us up here?" I guess if we waited long enough for the polar ice caps to melt then we'd be in business, but by then we'd all be living in a Kevin Costner's Waterworld and we might be susceptible to attacks from sea bandit smokers on jet skis, and those guys never got seasick.

If you're smart enough to think simple physics when visualising the ship moving through the water, then perhaps you will come to the conclusion that it might be best to find a seat somewhere in the middle of the ship where the motion isn't quite as intense. Also the lower the deck the better, so perhaps stay away from the aft or bow of the ship, and definitely keep out of the crow's nest. Now this may come as a surprise to some of you, but ships do actually bend in the middle, and in in the past have snapped in half because of bad weather conditions, no iceberg needed. The nautical term is hogging and sagging and is a catch 22 type situation. The smaller the ship the more it will get tossed around by the waves, but it won't bend or contort because it is shorter than the wave breaks. A huge ship with a hefty weight will not rock and roll as much as smaller vessels, but because it's longer than a lot of wave breaks, the ship can sometimes become vulnerable to twisting on one swell and hanging suspended between two swells either side of it. If you need a visual image to help you digest that mouthful then picture standing in the middle of a piece of suspended bamboo, the longer the piece is, the more it will bend. The bigger the ship, the more you will feel movement going on beneath your feet. If you stand directly in the middle you can actually feel your feet bend outward slightly in opposite directions (I am not joking). Now imagine being tucked up in bed nice and cosy in the middle of a large ship. All of a sudden the walls of your cabin violently rip outward (like how Moses parted the sea, but in this scenario your cabin is the sea, and it's in the sea!). Now all the chaos and destruction that the sea has to offer comes crashing through your room from both sides and underneath ... and above! (Why not, it's mental out there). It's like if the disasters of the Poseidon Adventure and the Titanic met the Perfect Storm, Jaws and Das Boot in a big ol' orgy, and somehow they had a baby, that baby is in your cabin, and boy is he angry. (That would be an amazing film to watch, I'd better get to work on the screenplay pronto). So basically, I guess what I'm trying to say is that while cruising is fun, it's not without its highly unlikely and overly exaggerated risks. So enter at your own, folks.

Some guests think that working on a cruise ship seven days a week for months on end is voluntary work experience, or a steppingstone to some dream job back on land. *So, what do you do for a real job?* was actually quite an annoyingly common question. Within the bubble of ship-life our existence is self-contained, we each have our place, our function, our role to play, but like everyone of course we want more out of life, it's human nature. Each day we wake up and we go about our duties to earn our pay cheque and always look to the future. To give an answer to that, my real job (whilst I was clearly at work) is a job in itself! I suspect that there probably is a job somewhere in the world, whereby the purpose of the role is to write up lists of jobs and put them into two separate piles each and every day. One pile is titled 'Real Jobs' and the other pile 'Not Real Jobs'. For example, Policeman? Real job. Titty wrangler? Not real job. Doctor? Real job. Masturbation teacher? Sorry, not a real job. The job of categorising other people's jobs does raise a lot of questions though. Who is the person doing this job and how did they get it? How do they know what goes into which pile? Who is this person's boss? What training did they go through in order to land this position? Which pile is their own job in? Does their job have benefits? Do they work on weekends? I could go on with this bit for a whole chapter, but the more I add to it the more ridiculous I feel. This is just mirrors reflecting mirrors in a never-ending reflection of ridiculous reflections being reflected ... reflectingly? I suppose the person who asked me what I do for a *real* job was thinking that my job was so much fun all the time that it couldn't possibly be considered work, so by their logic a *reeeeal job* is one where the work itself is boring.

I've moved on from cruises for some time now, but occasionally I might be scrolling through Facebook and see pictures posted by people I know who still work on them. I have mixed feelings when I see them, but I never think to myself, *when are they gonna finally get a real job?* because I know for a fact that it is real, and it is probably one of the realest jobs going. Every day is a different challenge, there are new places to visit and new people to deal with by the 1000s. My role was so varied that I was hardly ever bored at work, and I've had jobs in the 'real world' where I was counting down the clock till I could leave.

I honestly don't consider my time spent at sea as an extended vacation as some might think. It was full on! We worked hard, we played hard, burning the candle at both ends. What happened on the ship, stayed on the ship, unless of course someone like me decided to put it all in a book! I like to think, along with many other people, if you love what you do then you never work a day in your life. There are a lot of people doing jobs they hate because the need the money to support their families, but of course they love their family so much that they enjoy their work on some level. Then there are people who just love their work because it is awesome. I think most of us have experienced the weight of pulling all-nighters, trying to get some written work ready to meet a deadline, and then we were slapped in the face with the exciting lives of others via posts on Facebook. For me it was a great deal of people who were a constant source of distraction and envy, but one in particular is a guy I know who works for a stunts team. His job is to go and test obstacle courses for shows like Ninja Warrior. I regularly see posts from him off in some exotic location, swinging on this, jumping off that, having the time of his life basically. Some days I envy the shit out of him because he's doing something that I for one could never do, as I'm built for comfort not for speed, and also because I'd never heard of anyone else doing something like that as a career before. It looks like it's great fun, it pays well, and he gets to meet some pretty cool people. I've been on the dole before and I am somewhat ashamed to admit it, but never did I ever sit with a careers councillor and get presented with the option of flying around the world as an obstacle course tester. If I had been, I would have said yes in an instant, and started training for it immediately. Of course a lot of the best jobs aren't being advertised through the job centre, and obstacle course tester is no exception. The key thing to note here is that my friend is and always has been big on parkour. He not only tests these courses but he also uses his natural born agility to help choreograph stunts in films as a parkour consultant. So I'm very much at peace with the fact that he does something that I could never do, just like there are people out there who could never stand in front of an audience and host gameshows for large audiences like I do/did. We all have our strengths and some of us play to them better than others.

What do you do for a real job? The definition of 'real' in this context in undefinable, but the answer could and should always be *"What I'm best at."*

Chapter 5

Sometimes it's Time for Show Team Show Time

In my early days on-board as a lowly entertainment host it was often easy for me to feel physically inferior. This was all thanks to the incredible fitness levels of the in-house show team. Not only were they all in phenomenal shape but most of them could sing, dance and act which in show business is known as being a triple threat. I was barely able to stand confidently enough to create the illusion that I was in possession of a single threat, let alone multiple. I was still learning my craft and out of the entire crew I was the youngest person. Even though I was a part of the team, I often felt like I was on work experience. I was less a triple threat and more a multiple risk. All these show team members had gone to performing arts school and been at it since they were old enough to waddle. Each night they would perform high energy shows with amazing costumes, lighting and pyrotechnics. Meanwhile I'm next door standing in as dolly bird for Play Your Cards Right.

It's fair to say I was in awe of these super humans who I witnessed first-hand performing consistently to an exceptionally high standard. The girls were so warm and friendly but they were all the kind of girls who if they had been at my school would never have given me the time of day, nor would I have had the courage to speak to them. Most of the guys on the other hand were never really the kind of guys that I'd come into contact with at school. These guys were as gay and proud as the day is long. It was no secret, they were out there for all to see. For me this was the first time I had ever encountered guys who walked with sass, snapped their figures and strutted. Before I had a chance to figure out if I liked them or not, they disarmed me, infiltrated my personal space and quickly became my best friends. Reading that last sentence back I realise that sounds a little bit like something that may have happened behind closed doors, but I'm referring to their lack of respect for my personal space which came in the form of hugs and non-penetrative exchanges. I was assured by them that come contract's end I would become one of them, and even though I managed to avoid that predication from coming true, many of my friends back home in Essex deduced that because I had worked on a cruise ship, that made me automatically gay. During my stint on-board, if anyone back home was to ask any of my siblings, friends or relatives what I was up to these days, their response to, "He's working on a cruise ship" would be a slightly offensive high pitched, effeminate "Noooooo!" married with an *I'm a little teapot* pose.

You see out of everyone I knew growing up in Essex, I was the only one I was aware of who went on to do something within entertainment. I knew of a couple girls who went on to become dancers, but I didn't know any guys who were going down similar paths to my own. It's hard for me not to stereotype Essex, but in many ways it lives up to a lot of people's preconceived ideas. By default if you show any gravitation, natural proclivity or even predilection towards anything that could be considered 'the arts', then you might as well be labelled a fully-fledged drag queen diva. Things like a zero lack of interest in politics (except maybe the casual lean towards favouring UKIP policies), a love of fast cars, fast food, football, hair gel, aftershave, designer clothes, excessive lager drinking and occasional bit of violence, are just a few of the defining characteristics that make up the cheeky chappy, charming ladies' man, Essex boy stereotype.

If you know anything about me it's that I vehemently do not subscribe to this image. I prefer to think of myself as man of the people, a wherever I lay my hat kind of guy, although I have to admit, when a woman has asked me where I'm from, and her eyes have lit up because she loves the accent, I'd be lying if I said that I didn't play up to it from time to time ;) After all, we're all creatures of comfort, and what greater comfort is there than slipping into your natural speaking voice. However, being submerged in a culture throughout my entire childhood that subjectively lacks any real culture has, it's fair to say, rubbed off on me a little bit, dyanawhamean? I like to think I do my best to go against the grain. Not in an anarchistic sense but by going out of my way to try and do things differently. If ever I feel a particular way of saying, doing or even acting a certain way is starting to trend, I actively try to go the other way. I can't really explain it but I've always liked to find my own solutions and approaches to things instead of just doing what the majority seem to be going along with. When everyone goes along with something purely because it's deemed 'socially acceptable' that really grinds my gears. If I ever found a seemingly controversial trick or method that would enable me to be more efficient in getting some mundane task completed quicker, without even taking into account any social ramifications, I'd just get on with it and be proud that I managed to find a unique alternative without being told how I must do something. I wouldn't say I deliberately flaunt society's conventions like some smug know-it-all, and I also wouldn't say that I'm the kind of person who doesn't suffer fools gladly, because I do suffer fools gladly. I totally tolerate stupidity in others, because monkey see monkey do, and who doesn't love monkeys? Also, I love the idea of being pigeon-holed into a category of people, because it's the very idea of being categorically labelled that makes individuals strive for individuality ... individually, and without that we'd all just be a bunch of traditionalists traditionally being traditional because, well, it was tradition.

It seems that in the age we live in, now more than ever, a shortcut to individuality is to be able to coin a gimmick, something people can instantly associate you with. You could argue that this in turn renders the pursuit of striving for individuality rather pointless, because as soon as you achieve the goal of your ambition, you will inevitably be typecast by the very concept you were trying so hard to avoid in the first place.

The world of wrestling entertainment is littered with a plethora of individuals who have exploited every known trope, mimicked practically every profession and squeezed every last drop out of a metaphorical bottle labelled gimmicks. For example The Undertaker is a wrestler who undertakes the guise of a legitimate undertaker. This is a palatable and easily digestible gimmick for fans to accept, and over the years wrestlers have attempted to turn just about every profession going into a steroid-fuelled persona. Once they ran out of those it was time for them to up the ante and invent characters that had a penchant for reckless abandon, a fetish for the unimaginable or were even just mentally unstable. There was Martin 'Marty' Wright aka The Boogeyman, who smashed clocks and ate worms. There was William James Myers aka George 'The Animal' Steele, who had a green tongue and decided to eat turnbuckles (which are the pads in the corners of the ring). And who could forget the easily forgettable Fred Ottoman, aka The Shockmaster, who sported a Storm Trooper helmet sprayed silver and covered in glitter, with blue jeans and some weird furry coat thing to set the whole thing off.

One of the most profitable gimmicks of all time has to be Michael Buffer who makes stacks of cash as a ring announcer, uttering the words we all long to hear: "Let's get ready to ruuuuuumblllle!" Did you know that he makes more money on royalty payments alone than he does actually having to say those words, which is pretty fucking insane considering it was estimated he would make a tidy four mil for announcing the Anthony Joshua versus Wladimir Klitschko fight. It's impressive but on some level it does make you sick to your stomach.

I guess the sad truth is that the most profitable gimmick you can have is to exploit others', or to be affiliated with them - like a leech. I feel like that's basically what people like Vince McMahon, Michael Buffer and Simon Cowell are already doing.

Where was I? Oh yes, gay people. They tried to convert me, but this guy is unconvertable. To deliberately misquote Katy Perry, *I kissed a boy, and I did not like it*. A few jars too many may generally be the cause, and I imagine for a few of you, the morning after, many fragmented interactions have flashed before your eyes as you try your best to work out how your lips locked with a fellow liquored up lad. Like all men I know which side my bread is buttered. Normally it's a thick tasty wholemeal Hovis loaf with Lurpak lightest, and when I'm feeling cheeky, it's a freshly baked white tiger loaf with Lurpak slightly salted, Ooofff!

I have in the past often been asked if I am gay. This is probably because I am a bit of an extroverted performer type, and so some people might think that to mean I am gay. I have an ear for accents, I am not adverse to impersonating anyone, and my flamboyant homosexual is thoroughly convincing if I do say so myself (and I just want to be clear, I do not mean that I own a flamboyant homosexual who is thoroughly convincing, but that I do impersonate one rather well).

I've never really been the alpha male type and my capacity for violent sports is pretty much non-existent. Growing up, I was what you might call a late bloomer, and I never really had much confidence with women and I was pretty hopeless with them before I started on on-board. However, when I began working on ships, I was basically like a young Anthony Michael Hall in any 80's John Hughes movie, or I might even have been as bad as Dustin Diamond aka Screech from Saved by the Bell circa 1992. I couldn't see myself with any of the show girls at the beginning because to me, it was the equivalent of asking Kelly Kapowski to the dance. Every one of them were utterly gorgeous and completely out of my league. There were some pretty attractive girls that I had come into contact with during my education, but none of them could hold a candle to these girls. I remember being incredibly bashful whenever any of them would try to talk to me, and so news of my shyness quickly became well known. I was straight into the friend zone and out of the running for the role of potential viable boyfriend. Furthermore, it certainly didn't help my chances that my boss gave me the emasculating nickname 'Sammy-boy' which caught on like a virus. On top of that, my boss's boss said at a team meeting once that the show team are considered by the guests to be like Hollywood royalty, and the ents hosts are more like daytime Soap stars. This isn't an insult by any means, but in the context of the comparison given, the lesser of two compliments given at the same time does seem like a bit of a tongue in cheek insult.

The show team were an amorous lot as far as I could tell, but being just a wee lad who was yet to find the courage to mount a trusty stead, I might as well have been on duty for mucking out the stables. No I don't mean I was cleaning up after them, I just mean I was left behind whilst they all went out and galloped about frequently. You may have noticed that I'm trying my hardest here to dance around the subject, whilst I beat around the bush and dress it up in silly analogies, but you haven't yet gotten to the part where I put it in plain English. So here it is. On that, my first cruise contract, I and none of the stunning show team girls copped off in bunks to knock boots (I'm doing it again). Alright fine! I was nineteen, away from home, still a virgin and I didn't have sex. Also, the security was pretty watertight which meant no drugs were able to be snuck on- board.

So the first time I ever flew the nest was really quite the antithesis of sex, drugs, rock and roll. It was actually closer to masturbation, karaoke, and all you can eat buffet.

My next-door neighbours kept me up most nights because they had healthy late-night sexual appetites. I can laugh about it now but they both really put in quite a performance. If I was in that situation now there's no way I would have stayed silent. I'd be banging my fist against the wall shouting angrily until they stopped. I've always been very respectful when it comes to the noise levels made in the bedroom on my side of the wall, so I find it so very inconsiderate and rather unnecessary when others make it sound like they are walking on a hot beach. On the ship, one thing I should mention is that the walls are incredibly thin, almost paper width. So when the couple next door decided it's time for a late-night wrestle, not only was I treated to an audible experience, but a visual one as well. I could practically see the shapes of their bodies through the wall, and if I so wanted, document the many various positions for future reference. One time, when I was lucky enough to be treated to the sight of the woman's arse slamming in and out of the wall, I cheekily decided to give the surface area of the wall a playful little slap. The motion abruptly stopped and I heard her say, "Babe ... I felt something" to which the bloke modestly replied, "I should bloody well hope so, I'm going to town here!" The whole ordeal was really quite unbearable, and when it was finally all over I laid back in bed and sparked a fag myself.

Pathetically, the closest I ever got to any action was when I saw show team girls sunbathing nude. I'd never really sunbathed before, so the first time I did, I didn't know what factor I should be using. I was as white as a ghost and mistakenly applied a factor two sun oil, and by the end of the session I was a bright red lobster. That evening I made sure to wear my reddest shirts and ties so it would take away the attention from my burnt boat-race (that's cockney for face). I never made that sunbathing faux pa again and got into the habit of taking myself up to the crew deck to chill and unwind. If I was sitting in near proximity to the show team girls and they started chatting with me, my inner voice seemed to unconstructively yell, *JUST BE COOL! JUST BE TOTALLY COOL!* as if that would somehow help? When has anyone who tried to be cool ever just been cool? What is the rationale for this advice anyway? What is the end game or the hidden agenda behind it?

If I'm cool then maybe she will be comfortable around me, and if that happens then I'll get to keep looking at her boobs! Calm down, calm down, you're getting too excited! Maybe she'll got totally naked, maybe she'll need someone to rub sun cream all over her, maybe she'll be like, "Oh hey, I like the way you applied that lotion, how's about you and I continue this in my cabin?" Maybe things will get really hot and heavy, and we start dating and things get serious, so serious that we quit our jobs and go get a place together somewhere like Miami, there's a lot of boobs in Miami, what if I get caught looking at someone else's boobs and she leaves me?! Or! What if she asks me if I like the look of the girl I'm staring at, and suggests we go ask her if she's up for a threesome? And what if she says yes?! Will I be able to handle both of them at the same time and appease their amorous appetites?! Whilst all of this is going on inside my head, the girl is witnessing me clearly wrestle with the finer details of my fantasy. She decides that the awkward silence between us has been long enough to assume that I am indeed not cool, and so she should probably put her bikini back on. Dammit! Why couldn't I just be cool?!

There's something about being told to act casual or natural that puts an inordinate amount of pressure on a person. The first time I ever did extra work on a film, I was given the direction of simply walking casually down the street. Of course being new to the industry at that time, when I was told to do that I become overly conscious both outward and inward of how that was supposed to look. I began to over complicate things by questioning what my interpretation of a casual walk would look like, why was I being casual? Did I have something to hide? How casual is too casual? When does acting casual become nonchalant, and when does being too nonchalant begin to look like I'm just being lazy? With the cameras rolling, the pressure became too much, and I ended up walking like some kind of cowboy with rickets. Needless to say … it was far from casual.

At the end every show team performance, I and the other ents hosts would be on a duty known as show doors. This role had two reasons that justified it being in the work schedule. The first was to be there as the guests were exiting the lounge, to ask if they enjoyed the show and then quickly promote the upcoming show that we were about to do in the other lounge, and the second was to prevent anyone from lifting the backstage curtain and trying to get a sneaky peak of the boys and girls getting changed.

I kid you not some people have no concept of privacy and think that just because they spoke with one of the entertainment team briefly at lunch, this enables them to nip backstage to congratulate them on their performance. One guest even went as far as asking me how I got my jiggy jiggy on-board.

Sometimes the show team would be right there on the doors with us so that the guests could get pictures with them in their beautiful costumes. I would also be fielding the many questions from the guests along the way.

Now because there are more guests on-board than there are seats in any given lounge, the dinner service and show times are divided into first and second seating. This system is in place so that everyone has a chance to eat and see the main show, however guests are free to eat up on the lido deck, stay in their cabins or do whatever they like. I know I dedicated a whole chapter to foolishness so I'm sorry to do this to you, but a frequently asked question we got regarding this system was, "If we miss the second sitting dinner service then can we go to the first?" Imagine coming last in a race and asking the ref to pop you in first but for a different race completely, that's basically what that is!

One comment made by a disgruntled guest that really made me laugh, was a simple misunderstanding but it was nonetheless priceless. They bounded up to me after the show and collared me –

Guest: "Here! You said it was an Aladdin show! I was waiting the whole time for the genie to appear but he never did!"

Me: "No madam, you must have misheard me. I said it was a Latin show."

Some people just really got to have their Disney fix or else they get cranky.

It's a tough job being a show team performer. They have to be on point each and every night for not just one but two high energy shows. Regular circuit training and bi-monthly weigh-ins are common practice. This is so their body can keep up with the strain of performing and so their waistlines don't exceed their costumes. Sometimes a show's PG rating would get a sudden boost up the rankings if a dancer squeezed too tightly into their costume causing it to later burst open mid-show, or occasionally a bra might snag on something and get yanked off completely. Good times!

When the seas got a bit choppy, dance routines which included lifts would usually be cut from the show. The audience wouldn't notice though as they were too busy sliding back and forth in their seats across the highly polished floor. This in turn made the dancers laugh, which would make them break their concentration and forget that they weren't supposed to throw their partners up in the air. Or at least one dancer did. Ouch!

One thing to note about show team members is that most of them know how to stay well groomed. I don't know necessarily about the women (oh god why did I just say that!), but I shared my cabin with a fair few male show team members who were in total 89.5% gay. They told me that with all that dancing about on stage and quick costume changes, it was necessary for them to move around freely, and to be able slip in and out of complicated garments without the encumbrance of scratchy pubic hair. They would make statements such as: "Getting rid of it has changed my life!" and "I can't believe I ever lived with it to begin with."

So ... being the kind of person who's rather susceptible and easily sold on an idea (you're ahead of me aren't you!) I went forward with top-secret project deforestation.

The process sounded simple enough, but even the simplest of tasks can be poorly executed. I was told to head to the pharmacy and pick up a tube of something called Veet. You've probably heard of it. It's not some shady underground newly tested awaiting government approval wonder cream. People generally tend to know that Veet is a hair removal cream, whereas I on the other hand was totally oblivious. I went out into town, picked one up and strolled back to the ship. As I went, I bumped into many of the guests staying with us that week, who were unable to refrain from making some kind of passing remark on the contents of my shopping bag. No not because I was so naïve that I went around showing everyone what I'd bought, but because the shopping bag was practically transparent and sent out a clear message to everyone that I was about to get my hands dirty with some DIY gardening maintenance. Comments like "Oy oy sailor, getting a bit rough down there is it?" or, "You alright Sam, time to weed the garden is it?"

When I finally got back to my cabin it was go time. I won't be able to give you an accurate description, because luckily for you, I've forgotten. Whatever amount that was down there at the time was about to get liberated. So I slapped on a generous amount of cream and set a timer to let me know when to take it off again, but the timer never bloody went off! I must have had that stupid cream on for at least a whole ten minutes longer than was needed. Eventually, my body's natural alarm clock went off, when a tingling sensation began to stir in my private parts. This actually felt rather nice, for about ten seconds before sharply shifting from first gear into fifth and boy, was it agony! I raced to the bathroom, fumbled around frantically for the packaging, and I ripped it open to get my hands on the utensil designed for scraping the cream off. I glide … wait, what's the past tense of glide? Is it glid? Glade? No that's an air freshener. I just checked and it's glided which doesn't sound right to me. Slid is past tense of slide so why isn't it glid? Goddam I hate the English language sometimes. Anyway, I glided the scraper with ease straight through my once proud bush, like a blunt Spork through butter at room temperature. There was no resistance, just total and unquestionable cooperation. The end result? I was balder than the day I was born. It looked as though I'd been nuked and now nothing would ever grow there again (just in case you were wondering, it did, and when it grew back it was the spikiest, itchiest thing ever, so I wouldn't recommend it). I wasn't dancing around on stage all night so why did I need to do it in the first place?!

I never did it again for three reasons. It hurt in the removal process, it hurt during the process of growing back and it looked fucking ridiculous. It might have looked a bit bigger than usual because it was completely bare, but that wasn't a big enough positive for me to keep doing it because (and forgive me if I sound like I'm bragging) I don't have a penis complex. So these days I just trim.

I learnt a lot from the show team during my time at sea, not just lessons in pubic hair maintenance, but some good things as well. Yes a lot of them were a bunch of overly dramatic, overly sensitive divas and queens, but they also had so much of one trait that it actually began to rub off on me, and that was confidence. I was talking to women without sweating, coming into my own a bit more and just generally starting to have a bit more fun with people. They say that you are the average of the five people you spend the most time with, and so on some level I was an all-round entertainer. I may have not been the best at singing, dancing, hosting or DJ-ing, but I gave everything a go. In fact the only thing I probably excelled at was being average ... and do you know what happens when you excel at being average? You just get more average.

I tend to pretty much plateau at everything I try my hand at. My grades at school on average were C's, I'd never win any tournaments, but I also never go out in the first round. If it was me versus Joe Bloggs in a pay-per-view title match fight for Average Man of the World, then neither of us would win, because it would be a split draw decision based on points average. I've got an average I.Q, average looks, an average penis, average build ... I'm just average! Currently I'm averaging between ten to fourteen averages per minute which is more than average. I better slow it down.

If anyone should ask you how you are enjoying this book so far then please, try to avoid using the word average.

A few months into my first contract I moved into a cabin on the show team corridor which they had nicknamed Fluff Alley. I wish I could remember why we called it that but it's been over twelve years so forgive me. My best guess is that there might have been a lot of debris from feather boas floating about at some point, and someone came up with it. To live down there was like moving from Benefits Street to Hollywood 90210. Where I had lived before was in a dreary, dismal part of the ship, and the surrounding cabins were inhabited by crew, some of whom looked like they were on work release. On top of that, my cabin was located directly opposite the on-board morgue. Yes, you read that right. The ship had a morgue. A ship has to have a morgue otherwise where would you keep the dead bodies? The laundry department? The Galley? Bear in mind that people didn't die regularly on-board, and that the morgue was merely there just in case they did. I've got some stories about how people have died at sea but I'll save that for later. The morgue's presence at the end of my corridor genuinely freaked me out, so when I got the chance to move up the cabin/property ladder I was overjoyed.

It was never a dull moment on Fluff Alley as there was drama and japes aplenty.

One morning I woke up, rolled over and looked down at the floor to see my own reflection staring back at me. Then the ship shuddered and my reflection quivered which is when I realised that the room had flooded. A panic nearly swallowed me whole, but I quickly came to understand that there was no more water coming in. I gently woke up my roommate, who happened to be the biggest diva of all my roommates, and he went into full-blown panic mode screaming, "Help, HELP,

HEEEELLLP! SOMEONE SAVE US!" It was like I was sharing a room with Olive Oyl. When I managed to calm him down we hitched up our trousers and paddled to the corridor to find a waterlogged Fluff Alley. The neighbours were coming out of their cabins wearing their life jackets as a precautionary measure and who could blame them? Eventually some of the crew came over and reassured us that we weren't sinking. A pipe had just burst and there was no need to panic. I assessed the damage to the cabin - luckily there was none - and I was massively relieved that my roommate kept all his clothes under his bed, as this had absorbed most of the flooding.

When I think back to the morning I woke up to a flooded cabin, I often wonder how I would react if there ever was an actual emergency. I would like to think that I would be able to stay calm and perform my duties to the best of my ability. However that isn't a statement of fact as it has yet to be tested. Who knows how I would react when the proverbial shit hits the fan? Would I risk my own life by carrying the elderly from cabins ablaze? Would I heave flaming debris off of trapped toddlers? Would I exhibit balls of steel bravery and be a bedrock of courage for all to see? Or would I shit myself and hide in a barrel? Was the training I received prior to coming on-board going to be enough to help me tackle situations where life and death could be at stake? Probably not. I still reckon that I would have done my best to retain order in a worst case scenario. *BUT! If people started shouting at me and began clambering into the lifeboats in a frantic and disorganised manner, I would say, 'Oi, you, Noooooo!' à la Harry Enfield. Then I'd shoot up the place like First Officer Murdoch in Titanic. I'd mistakably misfire at Irish Tommy because he was pushed into me by someone else, apologies pal. Then I'd give Fabrizio a slap! Before he has a chance to call me bastardo, stumble on backwards contemplating the calamity of which I had contributed towards, then top me-self over the edge because I'm not an animal.* Something like that I suppose.

Luckily I never really had any physical entanglements with any of the guests on-board (by which I mean violence) however my cruise director, Stewart, wasn't so lucky.

One evening, there was a rather rowdy bunch of guests making noise in the front row throughout the whole of a show team's performance. As the show ended, Stewart closed the evening with a little speech, making a point of thanking <u>most</u> of the audience for holding their conversations until the end of the show, which was met with cheers and applause. Later, one of the guests from the noisy group confronted him in the toilet about his remark, and demanded an apology for making him look bad in front of everyone. Stewart attempted to explain himself rationally which the guest did not like, so he beat the shit out of him. Thankfully security were nearby to break it up, slap cuffs on the man and lock him in the brig. Stewart was bleeding all down the front of his shirt and was rushed to the doctor to be looked at. In the end he was okay but that story stays with me. It plays in the back of my mind when dealing with hecklers sometimes which is a bit troubling I'll admit. Fortunately I haven't suffered any kind of retaliation quite as bad as that one but I remain on my guard.

One of the stupidest heckles I've ever heard thrown at a comedian was, "Why are you so fat?" And the brilliant response: "Because every time I fuck your mum she feeds me cake." Now that's how you deal with hecklers. Genius! Thought I'd just throw that in there.

Another Comedian was not so much heckled but rather distraught that an audience member was asleep in the front row. He said to the man's wife, "Is that your husband asleep? Can you wake him up please?" she said she couldn't so he asked why, and she said because he's dead. He said well why didn't you do something yet, why didn't you inform someone? She said because she didn't want to spoil the show. I wonder how many comedians out there on the circuit have been asked how their show went, and were able to say they literally killed?

It's quite a known fact that the crew on-board a cruise ship is prone to the odd tipple. Ours was really no exception as everyone lit the candle at both ends and worked through their hangovers often. One place we used to go to and enjoy a couple of hippy vibes and a few drinks was in the crew mess late at night. The musicians would put on a little show in there and we would sing and clap along as they strummed their guitars. Not having enough instruments to go round we improvised with whatever we could find, a tube of Pringles with a few broken crisps at the bottom became an instant maraca. The general rule of thumb was that if you could bang it, shake it or scrape it then you were in the band. Other nights we held poker tournaments that sometimes went on until the morning sun came up. I had a fairly respectable talent for the game, and was given the poker nickname Sammy 'Nine lives' Catling, and as I had youth on my side and already knew my poker well, naturally I hustled them. So whenever I lay winning hands on the table I stuck with my childish act and pretended as though I didn't realise it was a particularly special hand. I find the trick is not to overdo it and gain the confidence of others before striking again.

As I mentioned before it was my job to socialise with the guests and that often meant having a drink with them. Typically work would finish at around midnight and we would sit with guests who had been kind enough to buy us drinks, or were happy to let us share the benefits of their all-inclusive drinks package. When the DJ started up I'd sometimes wind up doing shots with them, and then it wasn't long before I was down on the floor showing off some of my more experimental dance moves. When it was time for a change of scenery it was down to the crew bar to meet up with everyone. There was almost always something going on down there because if there was ever a reason for anyone to celebrate anything, then it wouldn't take much effort or planning for everyone to be involved. There were mostly birthday celebrations of course. Practically every other night it was someone's birthday and there were banners up and party vibes galore. If you needed a cake then it was easy to get one sorted for someone, so easy in fact that pretty much every night someone was blowing out candles on an identical cake brought up from the galley. People would theme their parties in an attempt to mix it up and make their party stand out from the rest. There was Hawaiian, Mexican, American, Limbo, Tikki, Toga and Pirate. Rock and Roll, Pimps and Hoes, Guys and Dolls, Geek Chic, Cowboys and Indians. 90s, 80s and 70s parties. A parties, B parties, C parties etc. To the A party I went as an arsehole. I don't know why I did this. I don't admire or condone the behaviour of arseholes, nor do I celebrate them in any way shape or form, but when it comes down to a choice between getting a cheap laugh that came from making a little bit of effort, or putting in loooads of effort and someone just going, "You look good!" I'll take the cheap laugh.

I found a cheap fake arse in some random novelty store, made some adjustments to it and attached it to my face. I even cut a hole in the middle and drew in some sphincter lines for authenticity. Then for my party trick I smoked a cigarette through my arsehole mask arsehole. What an arsehole!

Then there were engagements and anniversary parties, national holidays such as Indian Independence Day and Name days. This is when you celebrate the day of the year that is associated with your own name, but instead of receiving presents people often used to give them out. The crew bar was home to all once they had finished work. It could get pretty packed in there but it would stay open until 2 maybe 3am. Crew weren't allowed in passenger areas because of a 2am curfew that was enforced by the ship's security guards. If you were caught and didn't have a good reason then it could be an instant dismissal. If you got word of a cabin party going on after the crew bar had closed you could be sure it wouldn't stay secret for long. Every square inch of cabin space would be taken up by miscellaneous crew members who had found their way there. The gatherings would often be a mix of people from various departments on-board, and were always fun because when you opened the door to one it was a human lucky dip. Suddenly you'd see people who you hadn't previously seen in the same setting, cuddled up cosy next to each other laughing in a corner of someone's cabin. When and if security were called to investigate noise complaints at a cabin party, everyone would poke each other in the ribs and shush one another. The hive mind of the party would hold their breath and hope for the sound of footsteps to pass down the corridor without stopping. If the noise was too much to hide then we'd be shut down and have to return to our own rooms. As we exited, it probably looked like some sort of clown car circus routine and security would just stand in amazement as we walked by.

I mentioned earlier how rare the occasions were when we got to have an overnighter in port, even rarer was if you also had a reason to celebrate on this occasion. So in the event you should be in port overnight with a good enough reason to celebrate, you could more or less automatically go ahead and discount the next day. Everyone would know that you were about to go off the rails and come the next morning, you would be making a highly anticipated call up to the office stating that you didn't feel particularly well.

Who can blame anyone that goes out for a night of carnage on these occasions? Every night for months and months you have a total choice of three maybe four places you can go to of an evening. The passenger disco, the crew bar, a cabin party or if they have one a karaoke bar. I went out and had the time of my life on a couple overnights. The feeling was as though I'd been released from prison and I was allowed to go back into the real world.

Over the years I was on ships I think I had a grand total of four overnighters. One was in Palma de Mallorca where we had a great night out. Myself and a few show team members went to a club, danced all night, got smashed and I made out with a blonde Swedish girl (WHAHEEEY!). Another night I was out in Cairns and it was a similar kind of evening to Palma, except that it rained heavily and consistently all night so by the time we got back we were absolutely soaked, but I made out with an Australian (WHAHEEEY!). The third overnighter was in Dubai and was a long evening. We didn't manage to get off the ship until late and so we couldn't find a club, a live music bar or anything with an atmosphere open anywhere. Instead we gave up searching and went for food at a nice restaurant unanimously deciding that would be our enjoyment for the evening. We went to order some beer and wine for the table and was told, "Oh sorry there is no alcohol at this establishment." (NOOOOOOO!). We asked if there was anywhere else that would serve alcohol but nobody could give us any answers. It's probably not the most important thing that we didn't drink that evening as on-board we drank almost every single night anyway. So in comparison to a lot of other people's experiences on overnighters mine are incredibly sparse and tame.

One individual told me that around four or five in the morning when himself and the crew started heading back to the ship, they were so drunk they decided, once they could see the ship, to dive into the water and swim across the whole harbour fully clothed. They got on-board sopping wet, passing a no doubt very confused security guard on the gangway. I feel bad for Security, they have to put up with so much shit. They are the first faces you see when you get on and off the ship, meaning they are usually the first people guests direct their abuse towards. Their special power? They carry favour with the powers that be on-board, so they have the ability to see to it that you are dismissed if they feel so inclined. For this reason, it's probably a good idea not to wind them up too much.

Probably on many occasions crew members have come back to the ship from being out all night looking worse for wear. Then without a second thought security will target them to undergo a 'random' drug test, and before you know it, they've been fired with immediate effect, packed their bags and left without even the chance to say goodbye.

Luckily for me I've never been a big advocate for drugs, and thankfully none of my roommates were either.

Besides doing the big shows each evening the show team had other responsibilities as well. They would often help us with some of our activities, particularly bingo on sea days when the turnouts would be as big as the pot. With so many people in attendance my ACD Gary couldn't refuse to the opportunity to wind them all up. "Ladies and Gentlemen, I don't believe it! Seals! I'm actually seeing seals!" With those words everyone started running for the windows, pushing small children out of the way, knocking over tables and chairs all to get a glimpse of an animal they have all probably already seen before. With their faces pressed up against the glass and looking down at the ocean, Gary continued ... "Can you see them folks? They're there I'm telling you. Look carefully around the edge of the windows you'll see them. That's right folks ... window seals." Cue the biggest collective groan I have ever heard. This particular gag was something of a weekly routine and we all enjoyed seeing the passengers sprinting each time. Seals are not often spotted out in the middle of the ocean as they tend to swim near land, but the guests didn't know that, nor I for that matter the first time I heard the gag.

The show team also taught dance classes, ran ship tours, performed murder mystery plays and held hilarious fashion shows using only company branded clothing from the gift shop. Working with them was always fun and it brought the entertainment team closer together as a whole. In most cases we were like a big family. The majority of that family was known for being extroverts and divas so naturally there were upsets and arguments. We were usually able to overlook the things that annoyed us because no one held a perfect track record of exemplary behaviour, myself included. Living 24/7 in such close quarters became a challenge when hormones began to influence one another. The environment would often become quite tense at around the same time each month, so it became necessary to prepare for the oncoming storm and batten down the hatches. I'm referring of course to the women. After a few months of close knit living they would all start to surf the crimson wave or ride the cotton pony together. I'm speaking in idioms again. Periods! They were all on their periods! I didn't know such synchrony could happen so I did some research and found that there was a study in 1971 explaining the phenomenon as a defence mechanism. Mother Nature was kind enough to hand that one down to the ladies, and the purpose of this defence is so that female groups are sexually receptive at the same time. This is so they won't be singled out by men and therefore targeted. The male equivalent for those of you who are interested, is a term which has been dubbed 'irritable male syndrome'. This is when males experience irritability, nervousness and depression thanks to a drop in testosterone, but it is only really applicable to males in the animal kingdom as they would encounter the mood swings at the end of mating season, whereas us blokes don't really stick to the parameters of a mating season.

Perhaps the greatest daytime gameshow that we did up on deck was our tribute to 'I'm a Celebrity ... Get me Out of Here! (we switched out the word celebrity for entertainer). The show would consist of 6 contestants picked from the entertainment team, usually the ents hosts, show team, and if they were willing, the comedian guest act for the week. This show gave us the chance to sell ourselves to the audience and find out who among us was going over as the most popular. It really did get quite competitive at times and it would whip the audience into a frenzy. We would ham up the on-stage theatrics at every conceivable opportunity in a bid to try and get the audience on our side. There were a whole bunch of rounds that put us through our paces, each one designed to test a different area of our ability, such as speed, endurance, strength, flexibility and resourcefulness. At the end of a round we all sat blindfold in a row of chairs facing the audience. The host (usually Gary) would hold his hand over each of our heads in turn, and the person who received the lowest cheer from the audience would be eliminated. As we sat beside each other clueless as to who had been saved and who hadn't, we tightly held each other's hand for comfort as the audience started a backwards countdown from five. The tension of this moment was heightened by the fact that at the end of the countdown, a bucket of cold water would be thrown direct in our face. So now you get the picture. Each round someone else is eliminated until a winner is crowned. This individual would then be given the title of king or queen of the ship for the remainder of that cruise.

What fuelled the competition in us to win this game (besides a plastic crown) was the desire to be liked. Generally speaking though, whoever out of all of us had been on stage the most that week, would have made the biggest impression on the guests so would usually go on to win it. I never won it, let's just get that out of the way. I was hosting sporting events mostly, and only a few people would ever turn up, so my fan base was pretty slim in comparison to the other hosts who were on stage every night. No matter what gags I came up with and how much I battled to win at the events, I was never crowned king. All the rounds were physical, and bear in mind that I was up against show team members who were basically trained athletes, so what chance did I have!? It was clear I wasn't going to win the strength round because the male dancers were holding girls above their heads every night. I wasn't going to win the flexibility round because the girls could bend and twist their entire bodies like pipe cleaners. I'm not particularly resourceful, my endurance is shit, so that leaves the speed round which was my strongest by far. When I worked at Asda, I used to be the fastest checkout operator/trolley wrangler and basket collector there ever was. I even used to speak so fast that I had to have elocution lessons to learn how to slow … it … down. In any case we're all familiar with the story of the tortoise and the hare, so I didn't win the speed round either! That left me with no other option but to do the only thing that I did well, which was play the sympathy card. At best this got me into the final round if I was being particularly pathetic, but it still wasn't enough to get me that crown. It was only when my parents came on-board for the week that I finally managed to claim a victory. It may well have been entirely because the audience knew my parents were watching, which kind of made me more of a social enterprise, but I didn't care, I had finally won. Screw you, show team!

Chapter 6

What Happened Next?!

Alright calm down let me tell you.

Now my first ever contract was to be 6 months long, and three months in I discovered what is known as the mid-contract blues. This is when you come to the realisation that the whole time you have been away from friends and family back home, has only been around half the time you still have left of your contract. When my six month contract was nearing its end, I was offered the choice to stay on board and extend it to ten months. I didn't really give it much thought, and agreed almost instantly. When I saw my fellow ents hosts leave I was in floods of tears (God I really was a wimp back then). The thought of them leaving after all the memories we had shared together got me really sad, and the task of having to start an entirely new friendship from scratch with a bunch of new guys seemed exhausting. My first team will always hold a special place in my heart as they were the first ones to help me find my voice on the microphone and believe in me. So for that I thank you. My team's replacements however were also great. We had lots of fun together if not more than I had with the previous team. In Barcelona we always found something different to do. We went to possibly the world's worst waxwork museum, which I remember had a life size model of Luke Skywalker, with a face that looked like a 6-year-old girl who had melted. We took in the stunning architecture around the city, explored Nou Camp (Barcelona FC's home ground), watched street performers on Las Ramblas, ate at the Hard Rock Café, drank at a bar that was themed as a fairy woodland and visited the sex shop of course. They had everything in that place, and I mean everything. They even had a live sex show right in the middle of the shop floor. Obviously it wasn't out on open display, you had to step into this little booth via a door. Before you go making assumptions that I'm some kind of pervert, I didn't go in there alone, I went in with a friend. We didn't do anything naughty we were just curious, alright! Inside the booth (brace yourselves) was a big black leather chair, a box of tissues and a small rubbish bin which was nearly brimming over. On the wall in front of you was a coin slot which took only one euro coins. A euro got you 100 seconds on a clock counter, and once you'd paid, a small blind began to raise on a window in front of you. What was revealed in this room was a circular bed slowly rotating, with either a live strip tease or full on sex show taking place. The idea itself isn't bad, however the architectural concept is in need of a serious rethink. The problem was that the other booths you could go in formed a circle around the room where the show took place. So once you're able to see inside, you can also see the sweaty faces of the other patrons pressed up against the glass. This rather off-putting imagery was more than I had bargained for so I left the booth, then I thought to myself who the hell has the job of cleaning up in there?! I mean I get that leather upholstery is the obvious choice, but who would ever agree to that as one of their duties? People cum and go as they please (sorry) and then some poor bugger has the responsibility of swabbing smelly semen out of slimy sofas. Euuurrgh … let's move on shall we.

Shopping is great in Barcelona, each time we were there the temptation to buy a new outfit or gadget was hard to resist. The big supermarket Carrefour was a great place to pick up all your cabin snacks and consumables, and as an added bonus, the checkout runners were all beautiful girls in tight fitting uniforms wearing roller skates. As they glided effortlessly along it made me really want a pair of my own, so I headed to the department store El Corte Ingles to treat myself. I couldn't wait to try them out so I literally put them on as soon as I'd paid for them. The motivation behind buying them was primarily for fitness, because I'd been getting a bit greedy with the buffets lately and a pot belly was starting to show. Plus the pavements were smooth around Barcelona, so it seemed like the perfect place to skate. After I bought them I went off to stretch my legs and get my heart rate going. It wasn't long before I realised that I was somewhat lost. I had to ask strangers for directions to the port, and no-one knew what I meant. So I tried adding an O on the end because that made sense somehow. "El porto?" I said. "Que?" they replied. It's not a million miles away from the actual word I should have said which I now know is puerto, but I literally asked like twenty people that afternoon, and they all shared the same look of confusion. I was in a mad rush to get back to the ship because I was supposed to be hosting an afternoon quiz up on deck. When I finally got back on-board I kicked off my skates with much relief, as they had given me rather severe blisters. I crawled up to the top deck to see Stewart waiting there, with his arms folded and a less than pleased expression slapped on his face. I grabbed the mic and started immediately, trying to catch my breath at the same time. I had been so stressed about missing my quiz because I was finally getting the opportunity to host by myself, so I wanted to prove to everyone that I was up to it and could keep an audience entertained. Annoyingly only three people turned up to my quiz that afternoon, and they sucked the fun out of it because they all took it so seriously.

That evening I got really drunk. I remember feeling like I was stuck in a rut and was making no progress, so I decided to drown my feelings with alcohol. Hardly ever does anything good happen when you lose self-control, but this was not one of those occasions. It seemed I had a touch more sexual magnetism than I thought, because that evening the Hungarian lounge band singer decided to come on to me. Apparently she had a thing for me and everyone knew about it. She had been sending me signals but being an oblivious virgin I had no idea what those signs were, or what they were supposed to indicate. SO! We found our way back to my cabin and that's when I lost my virginity. I'm not going to go into detail about it, there's no need to. All I'll say is that I was extremely drunk, I barely remember it, but I do remember her asking me if it was my first time. Of course I lied and said no, but I think she definitely knew. The most awkward thing about the evening was not the sex itself, but rather the situation. As we crashed through the cabin door we were practically tearing each other's clothes off, and sitting at the desk playing a video game was my roommate. He looked at us for a moment and then without saying a word he just turned back to his game, put on some headphones and continued playing. We had drawn a curtain around the bed so we had some privacy but it was still a bit odd to be intimate with someone for the first time whilst someone else was sitting a metre away. What was terrible about the situation, and I swear I did not know this, was apparently my roommate was head over heels for this Hungarian honey. He had taken her out for dinner and drinks, bought her flowers, announced how he had strong feelings for her, but she didn't return them. Instead she did the tacky thing of sleeping with his roommate whilst he was in the room. Had I known any of this information at the time then of course I would never have gone through with it, but I didn't. So the next morning I was strutting around with a smug smile on my face, proud that I'd finally left boyhood behind. When I was informed later that very same day about her behaviour I was lost for words. I was no longer proud of myself and instead just felt kind of used and cheap. Nothing stays a secret for long, I mentioned that already, so when word got out about me and the Hungarian, people were torn in their decision to either comfort my roommate, or congratulate me on losing my V plates. The main reason nothing stays a secret is because there is no possible way of doing the walk of shame without being spotted. She was seen returning to her room in last night's clothes, which was all that was necessary for anyone to get their much-needed dosage of daily gossip.

The culture of social interaction with ship life is sort of like a mixture between secondary school and prison. Everyone discusses everyone just like they do at school, but we all lived together so in that sense I liken it to being in prison. Relationships are never private, everyone knows who is whose bitch (or to put it in softer terms who wears the trousers). The dating process tends to accelerate quicker because you are with them all the time, so a two-week relationship on-board would be equal to two months on land. If you were lucky enough to have your own cabin then you had it made. Girls would be more inclined to see you as potential boyfriend material, simply because they knew they could be intimate without any interruptions.

Regardless of being made to feel like I was a sex puppet having his strings pulled, I actually gained a lot of confidence with women from that point on. This is probably because a lot of conversation with alpha male types is typically about sex. So now that I was able to join in with the banter I finally felt as though I had become one of the lads.

Lad culture is a big part of Essex life, so it's understandable that losing my virginity would help me find some relief in being able to return to my native homeland and announce that I had earned the rank of lad. In a further attempt to solidify my newfound title, I had a great business idea which is to start a fast food vegetarian restaurant chain that targets the lad demographic. I've called it 'Quorn, Son!'

Of course the harder you try to be a lad, the less likely you are to actually be one. In my opinion if you habitually share Lad Bible style posts on social media, then that's pretty telling that you desire above all things to be seen as one, which by default means that you aren't. Well, unless you're in the video you shared, then it's arguable that you might be.

I once had a conversation with an Italian guy who asked me to help him understand what the difference was between being a lad and a bloke. So I told him that typically a lad is a younger man who goes out drinking with his mates and chases after women each night, whereas a bloke is someone who has settled down, is occasionally spotted down the pub, but generally no longer needs to go out on the pull. Ironically it is usually a bloke who has to explain what the definition of a lad is to a lad. After I had given this explanation the follow up question was "So what is a pal"? I told him a pal is like a friend, a mate, a buddy, a chum. He said, "So could I say this is my pal if I was introducing a friend?" I said yeah sure. "Well could I say this is my lad?" No that would mean he was your son. "Could I say this is my bloke?" No that would mean that you're gay. The English language must be so confusing to learn sometimes.

At the start of each week when the new passengers came through the terminal. We would often check out the fresh talent that was coming aboard, and I remember the word 'phwoaar' was used a lot. Part of being a newly accepted lad was that I could finally partake in this tradition. We were discreet for the most part, obviously we didn't want to give the guests a terrible first impression.

It's worth mentioning at this point that sleeping with guests is strictly forbidden and is an instant sackable offense, but that's only if you're silly enough to get caught. If you hit it off with a guest then of course it's only natural that the two of you would want to find somewhere quiet and secluded to talk, and this would be yours or their cabin. Getting past security undetected became a sneaky stealth mission, but it's worth it because forbidden love is always more exciting.

By the time my folks came on-board to visit I was eight months into my first contract, and had become a man at least twice. It was the longest I'd ever gone without seeing them, and sure enough when I greeted them at the gangway my mum burst into tears again (I guess I really am my mother's son).

Having them with me for the week was nice and made me feel somewhat guilty that I hadn't been the best at keeping in touch as regularly as I could have done. It's not that I forgot about them, how could I? Mum would send me a shoebox every now and then which was full of home comforts. She really ticked all the right boxes that one would expect to see on a highly qualified and fully accredited mum CV. She would put in things that she thought I would need like a new inhaler, eczema cream, sun cream, handwritten letters from home, and a CD mix of new music that she thought I'd like. In addition to these thoughtful gestures, she'd put in my favourites snacks which included the likes of nice 'n' spicy Nik Naks, pickled onion Monster Munch, Quavers or Wotsits (I'm a firm believer that the stinkier the crisp, the better). Of the chocolate variety there were a mixture of Curly Wurlys, Crunchies, Double Deckers, Lion Bars, Boosts and McVitie's gold bars (I also believe that the stinkier the chocolate bar, the worse). Sometimes though, the box would have been handled a bit too roughly for my poorly protected perishables and so would sometimes arrive a bit broken and melted, or the crisp packet would have been split and therefore turned the crisps stale. Of course I couldn't complain, I still ate everything because they were a rare currency on-board like smokes are in prison, and the rationale behind rationing my rations was I thought rather rational.

It was difficult at times to keep them to myself, because colleagues would get a whiff of them as they passed my cabin sometimes and be like, "Sam are you eating Monster Munch?! Ahh give us pack!" I wasn't altogether stingy with my home treats, but I also wasn't Morgan Freeman in Shawshank, meaning I wasn't the guy inside who could get it for you. I was simply just a young adolescent happily sitting on the receiving end of his mother's long distance mollycoddling.

I expect that because my brother had already shacked up outside the nest with his long-term girlfriend, and because my sister was soon to be going to uni, mum was doing all that she could to still feel like a mother, and I was more than happy to cash in. When she came on-board though, I had done a lot of growing up since leaving and was no longer the young clueless son who waved goodbye to her at the airport. I was hardly unrecognisable to them, as all that had really changed about my appearance was that I now had a thin layer of peach fuzz around my chin and lips, nevertheless, when I saw Mum for the first time I had to do that thing all men do, which is to supress the urge to go running up to mummy for cuddles and kisses, and instead act as though you haven't missed them at all. It didn't matter that I tried to be totally nonchalant, as Mum did more than enough to make a scene worthy of embarrassment all on her own, by wrapping her arms around me, and attacking me with a barrage of pecking kisses all over my face. I gave my sister an awkward hug because for some reason she has problems with intimacy around me, and I gave my dad the obligatory *how's it going, old man?* pat on the back. I showed them to their rooms, gave them their own personal tour and left them to settle in. The following day we made plans to go out and about around Villefranche, visiting Nice, Monaco and Monte Carlo. It was a long hot and tiring day, but we saw some amazing things, beautiful scenery and expensive stuff. They really know how to shove their wealth and success in your face down there, so if you're the jealous type then take my advice, don't go, you will just feel like a failure.

As we walked along the sea front marvelling at the yachts and super cars, we decided to stop off for a coffee. It was at this time I decided to be forthcoming with my family and come clean about my newfound addiction, smoking. To my surprise they were actually pretty cool with it. For them to have tried to lecture me at that point would have been hypocritical, because they had both smoked when they were of a similar age, and my dad was actually a secret smoker for about ten years. Whenever he came home from work he would always smell of smoke. If Mum asked if he'd been smoking, he would normally say something like, "No I just popped

into the pub on the way back for an orange juice, dear."
This being well before the smoking ban in 2006, dad
could obviously use this excuse, today however, no
way!

Anyway, so with my parents blessing I got out my
pouch of Golden Virginia and proceeded to roll my
own, which actually impressed my parents more than
anything, as they were pleased to see that at least I was
old school. As we sat down for coffee, I lit a cigarette
and I told them how I came to start smoking.

Basically the ship's predominant nationality for officers
on-board was Greek. For those of you who don't know,
a traditional Greek breakfast is coffee and a cigarette.
This information is somewhat irrelevant but it's just an
indication of the smoking culture that I was subjected
to. In the evenings the officers' bar was thick with
smoke. It was almost as bad as the glass smoking rooms
you get at airports once you've gone through security.
Those rooms are glass hot-boxes of death. You go in to
smoke your own cigarette, but before you've even lit
one you've inhaled the equivalent of around ten to
fifteen fags, so you no longer want one. In the officers'
bar however the smell of tobacco grew on me, and I
came round to it in the end. *And so, Mum and Dad,
that's sort of why I smoke now*. Mum's response was
rather unexpected, because I had been speaking about
the origins of starting to smoke, I wasn't actually doing
much smoking. Mum had clocked this and also noted
how I was holding my cigarette, which was, according

to her generation, 'a bit gay', so she said, "Yeah, alright, whatever, are you gonna smoke that or what, you big poof?" I had no defence for the way I held my cigarette, except that maybe I'd been hanging out with the show team boys too much. Who knows!

Having friends or family visiting does have its advantages, as you get to take extra time off work to go and explore. You also have the added experience and privilege of eating in the restaurant on-board, instead of the crew mess night after night. It was in the restaurant that I tried escargot in garlic butter for the first time. This is snails, people! Slimy, slippery, saucy, squelching snails! They were actually quite nice if I'm honest, but no matter how you dress it up to try and make it look and sound more appealing, the image of a snails eyes atop waving tentacles whilst they crawl along leaving a trail of slime constantly played through my mind, and overall ruined the experience.

Tables in the restaurant are prearranged so that everyone gets a seat, this means that you have to sit at the same table each night, and you had better hope that the people you are sitting with are easy going. We got lucky on this occasion, but I've had other times where I'd scarf my food down as quickly as possible so I could get away. The waiters make a tremendous effort to give you the very best service every time, and you generally have the same waiter each night so it's nice to be able to give a tip to someone who has literally fed you all week long.

At some point during the cruise all the waiters put on a bit of a show. This is their time to shine and they really go for it. Some of them even give the show team a run for their money. They sing, they dance, they play instruments, and they get the guests to clap and cheer along. I know it sounds like a tacky night out at T.G.I Fridays, but it's a lot classier than that ... trust me.

Having my parents with me, I really got to have a partial taste of what it felt like to be a guest on-board. I had a significant reduction in my workload, which meant more time to go out for some all-day excursions. In a weird way it felt like my parents had come to visit me in prison, and I was able to walk with them outside the confines of the prison yard unsupervised. I'm definitely over exaggerating, but I was more relaxed going out for the day, exploring further than I had done before, because I wasn't rushing back to the ship to run an activity.

When the time came for my family to leave - you guessed it - Mum gave us yet more tears. Yes it had been a lovely week and we had shared some happy times together, but for Christ's sake, Mum, why can you never just hold it together? It being the first time I had seen them in eight months the way we all treated each other felt totally different. For starters there were a lot less arguments between us, and I got the feeling that they were speaking to me a bit more like an adult. I guess it's because they didn't want to make me feel like a child in a big boy's world. They had been thoroughly supportive throughout their stay, and their presence at the evening entertainment helped to boost my fan club numbers which gave me a bit of added confidence.

I was sad to see them off of course, but if I'm honest by that point a small part of me just wanted to see them go. I say 'them' when actually it was more just my mum (sorry Mum but that is true). The sheer intensity of her mothering had just gotten to be too much. It was like she was dropping me off to stay the night at a friend's house, and she was making a fuss and outstaying her welcome. *He likes it when you stroke his hair and has to be in bed no later than 10:30, make sure he brushes his teeth and no sweets after 8pm. If he's feeling chesty here's his inhaler, if he gets itchy here's his cream, and if he can't stop sneezing here's an antihistamine...* Then to top it all off she'd do that thing mothers do - lick her thumb and try to rub some invisible mark off my face. I'd had the sweet taste of independence and now was now being dragged back to dependency. *Cut the cord mum, I'll be back home in two months.*

Chapter 7

The Importance of Down Time

With a demanding seven day a week schedule it's crucial to be in firm control of one's own down time. This means getting the most out of your freedom in as small amount of time as possible. As I mentioned previously, I quickly became quite adept in the art of napping. Necessity is the mother of invention, and when it comes to serious sleep deprivation as a result of constantly working, napping is less of a life choice and more a daily essential. Whether it's just flopping fully clothed onto your bunk and shutting your eyes for five minutes, or stripping off completely, getting under the covers and drawing the curtains around the edge of your bed to get some much needed peace and quiet for an hour, you had to do it because before long you would have to re-emerge back into passenger areas for the next fun-filled, energised activity. If you were living in an inside cabin, as soon as you turned out the lights it was absolute pitch black which made falling asleep all the more easier.

Every cabin is equipped with a phone and it only ever seemed to ring when I was napping. To make matters even worse it clanged like an industrial fire alarm which gave me a heart attack every time. As all the people I knew basically lived next door, we didn't really bother to use our phones to call one another, so there was really only one reason why anyone would be calling, and that was if we were supposed to be somewhere that we weren't. I became accustomed to being woken up by the phone, rolling over, picking it up and putting it to my ear, only to have someone on the other end yelling, "Sam where are you?! You're supposed to be hosting rope quoits!" This cyclic routine was in need of correctional behaviour ASAP, so the next time I was asleep and the phone rang I wouldn't answer it. Instead I hurriedly got dressed, and rushed upstairs hoping not to bump into anyone who I might get into trouble with. If I had to explain myself for being late, I might have to improvise an excuse with something like, "Oh I'm really sorry I was helping a guest find their lost child…"

On one occasion when I heard my phone ring, I immediately jumped out of bed and saw that it was three o'clock. I thought, *Shit I'm in so much trouble as I've missed like four duties*. I got changed and rushed upstairs as quickly possible, only to find that there was absolutely no one around. It was when I eventually looked out of a porthole that the penny finally dropped. It was three in the morning, not the afternoon. Had I been living in a cabin with my own porthole this situation would probably never have occurred.

Having such an obnoxiously loud phone does put you on edge a little. It was a ticking time bomb that jolted you upright, and made you smack your head on the top bunk or ceiling every time it sounded. If you saw another crew member walking around with a ridged dent in their forehead, chances are the cabin phone wake-up call was the culprit.

Each cabin also came with a TV. On some ships there would be a channel that displayed a direct link to a camera that sat on the bridge looking out across the bow. This was mostly for the benefit of those of us who were in inside cabins and wanted to check what the weather was like outside. Additionally the TVs would play movies, but they would be the same movies stuck on repeat, day after day, week after week. I guess who-ever was in charge of the movie schedule fell asleep with his cabin phone off the hook, smart guy. So it was each man for himself when it came to home entertainment. This was at a time before the invention of smartphones, and Wi-Fi was not free. If I remember correctly it was around twenty pounds for three and a half hours of internet, and the connection was a bit crap. So everyone would have DVD cases packed to the brim, or if they were a bit more tech savvy they'd have an external hard drive with a bunch of movies on them. Films in whatever form became a sort of trading card currency on-board. Either you'd flick through your neighbour's DVD book, or scroll your mouse wheel through their external hard-drive files *got, got, got, seen, got, NEED!* I'll admit that I probably watch too much TV, and every time I get close to checking everything off my watch list, a bunch more get added and it never ends. So in a desperate attempt to get through more films and shows than the average human, I sometimes watch things on VLC media player in times two speed with subtitles. It might not be the way the director intended for me to view their film, but at least I saw it and crossed it off my list.

Not being able to surf the World Wide Web, watch the news and keep up to date with current events, we had to make do with whatever resources were available to us and thus the art of binge watching was perfected. Should our laptops breakdown on us then naturally general panic ensued. If we didn't have our laptops it felt as though a little piece of our souls had been taken away from us. One of my colleagues had a particularly rough week as one rocky night, a bottle of sun cream fell off his shelf and on to his laptop below. This of course rendered the device useless so he had to buy a new one. The next day in Naples, he was walking through town and saw some guys selling laptops right there on the street. He thought he had found the deal of the century so he went to a cash machine to make a withdrawal, he raced back to the men, handed over the cash and received a box in return. When he got back to the ship and opened it up, he realised they had pulled the ol' switcheroo on him, and all that was inside was a loose bag of sand. We all felt so bad for him that we had a whip round, and tried to raise the funds to help him recoup his loses. The lesson here of course is never buy anything of any value on the streets of Naples.

It cannot be stated enough that everyone working onboard works hard. One thing that makes a contract better is the crew's ability to help each other out in whatever way they can. This doesn't necessarily mean that the crew has adopted a mafia like mentality, whereby you scratch my back, and I scratch yours. You should bear in mind that everyone is essentially working in hospitality, and they wouldn't have taken a job in that environment if they didn't have some keen desire to help people in the first place, and, at work, who above all people do we aspire to make the happiest? My belief is that for most of us, those people are our colleagues, and this is especially true in an environment like a cruise ship, because you are with them all the time. In an office you might be less inclined to be courteous as you might just want to punch in and punch out so you can go home and get on with your life, but it could not be more different on a ship. It's an unspoken rule that you all hold equal shares in making work the best place it can be. Now I know I said this didn't mean it operates like the Mafia, but in a way it sort of did. Crew are more than happy to help each other if they are able to, but they ultimately would like something in return if it can be extended as a polite gesture. It's not enforced, but it is sometimes expected. Each of us has access to something that has some monetary value that can be exchanged for goods and services. It goes back to the prison yard/cigarette analogy I guess. For example as an entertainer I had a key to the locker which held all of our game show props, quiz cards, costumes and of course prizes. I'm not talking big cash giveaways, I'm talking company branded keyrings, pens, medals and sometimes even little plastic cruise ship trophies. So a few fell out of my pocket from time to time (wink wink nudge nudge) and if someone sees that someone else has got one then they all want one too. Within reason I didn't mind of course. Why should the guests be the only ones to be able to get their hands on these coveted prizes? The way I saw it, we had to order in stock now and then whenever we were running low, and they were delivered in huge boxes heaving with cheap plastic or metal doodads, which were then given away over the course of the next few weeks or months. I wasn't skipping down the crew corridors tossing away great big handfuls singing *"FREE PRIZES!"*. No, now and again, I would just give some to those who were discreet enough to keep it to themselves. We had a budget to stick to after all.

God I've properly just incriminated myself. I may now have to do some time in the nick. This story is my tell all after all. I'm just being honest about the ins and outs of *quid pro quo* on-board. I know that my wife would be absolutely furious to hear that I pulled off this kind behaviour. She's South Korean and believes there's a right and a wrong, and no grey area in between. She says to me, "Sam, we have a strong belief in Korea, you shouldn't take what doesn't belong to you. You could leave your wallet in the street, come back at the end of the day and it would still be there. We have a saying that if you see a penny in the street you can't have it because it doesn't belong to you". Normally the wife is always right but in this case I couldn't resist the chance to counter with our culture's belief. "We have a similar saying," I told her. "Find a penny, pick it up, and all day long you'll have good luck." "Noooooo, it's very bad luck, Sam!" she said.

She's so upstanding, my wife, I don't know why she doesn't just apply to become an environmental enforcement officer. These uniformed do-gooders are unaffiliated with the police, and are a private firm outsourced by the council. They get their salary directly from commissions earned from penalty payments, so I reckon if my wife used her OCD for good, she could make an absolute killing. To give you an idea of how strict she is on me, we were out shopping one day, and I was looking for a toiletry product, but didn't know which one specifically. So I lifted the cap on one of the products and squeezed less than a petit-pois-sized portion on the tip of my finger to test its smell and viscosity. She doesn't believe in try before you buy so she forced me to buy it, and in case you're wondering, I didn't break a foil seal of any kind, I just lifted the cap. I'm not an animal! You would think that I would have learnt my lesson by that point, but no, I didn't. When I was paying at the self-service checkout I didn't declare the two 5p carrier bags that I had used because I was annoyed I was being made to pay for an item that I didn't even really want. She saw me do it, and didn't talk to me for the rest of the day.

Where was I? Oh yeah - *"FREE PRIZES!"* So I wouldn't give them away to every single person who asked. I'd have to let them know I was running low and didn't have any spare. If I did give stuff away it was either because I was feeling generous, or cheekily wanted something in return.

There are a lot of different departments on-board, and out of those departments there are a select few who it's smart to be on good terms with. If you curry favour with the bar staff they might just add the odd extra shot so you can actually taste the alcohol, or they'll slip you drinks via a guest's all-inclusive card without them knowing, which is cheeky yes I know, but it doesn't really make a difference because it's already paid for.

If you are hosting a cabin party then having Security on your side is a definite must! Whether it's offering them a cigarette, a drink, or a trophy. Treat these guys like they are just late to the party and are welcome to come inside and put their feet up as they work the longest hours out of everybody. In return they won't send everyone back to their rooms, they will just ask that you keep it down a bit and will often let you continue your party.

Just like the guest rooms, every crew cabin has a housekeeper tending to it daily. So obviously take good care of your housekeeper, and they will take care of your room. If you tip well enough, your laundry will be hanging back outside your door not long after it's been taken away. Like security, housekeepers work crazy long hours and they deserve every penny they get.

If you want to go on some organised trips for free then you need to put yourself forward to the shore excursion team. If you actually get to go can often be potluck because anyone who gets a bit of time off is always trying to tag along on an excursion for the day. This makes getting a place rather difficult, but becoming friends with the shore ex dept can only help your chances when trying to secure that last available seat on the coach. To ensure that I was a favourable choice for going on these excursions, I often brought back souvenirs, leaflets, customer feedback, whatever I could to help the team get a fuller picture of the trips they were selling.

The salon girls (referred to by the crew as Steiner's, because that's the corporation that hires them) work long hours on terrible commission structures. If you play your cards right though you can get discounted or sometimes even free treatments! Haircuts and massages mostly, and who doesn't love getting a free massage? One unforgettable image I have is seeing a rather unlikely patron of the salon whenever I walked past. He was a broad shouldered, hairy forearmed, surly looking officer who would often be sitting in the chair getting manicures, pedicures and facials. This made me think there's no shame in trying to stay on top of grooming oneself in an attempt to become a modern man, so I decided to book myself in for a treatment and have my ears candled. This is when you lay down on your side and they stick a lit candle in your lughole. The flame draws out the wax through the ear canal and into the candle. You can then see for yourself a lifetime's worth of build-up collected in one place. When I stood up after the treatment and said thank you, my first realisation was, *Oh my god I'm this loud?!* I never had a particular problem with my hearing, but after having that treatment I noticed the precise pitch of my patter projecting from my pie hole couldn't hurt to be lowered.

All in all, be nice to the crew, heck - be nice to people! It goes without saying that this advice is common sense to most of you, but if you wonder why you never get the customer service you feel you deserve ... it's probably because you're a bit of a dick.

Chapter 8

A Few of My Favourite Things

With so much work on-board to keep you busy, and so many fun activities to look forward to, it can leave you rather spoilt for choice. Over the next few pages I want to focus on some of the things that at the time I took for granted, but now look back on with utmost fondness. This is because either I miss the convenience of those things, or simply miss them being a part of my day to day routine. Take for example the daily commute. If you rely on trains and buses each day instead of driving yourself in, then they normally offer us the chance to catch up on sleep, news, gaming, work or TV and films. I think most people would agree that if they lived closer to their place of work they would probably set their alarms to a later time so they could sleep a little bit longer, and those who live further away have no choice but to get up that hour or so earlier. Ironically it is usually those who live closest to work that end up being late because they cut it too fine and don't think there's a possibility of them being late. On a ship however there is no commute time, because you don't get to leave until your contract ends. This means that quite often I fell into the routine of setting my alarm as close to my starting time as possible, as I didn't have to worry about hitting traffic on the journey in. Each to their own I suppose. Some people love commuting in the mornings, especially those driving because they can listen to the radio without headphones, sing loudly and generally just shout abuse at other motorists. If you do any of those things in a packed carriage underground at seven in the AM, then people don't usually look too pleased. In society today everyone treats the morning commute as something that they have to do, and would like to get over and done with, with as little drama as possible. They definitely don't feel that it's necessary to be striding through the open first thing, shaking maracas and singing Build Me up, Buttercup at the top of their lungs. Being packed underground like canned sardines when you're on the grind is hard enough without that sort of nonsense to deal with. So to work on-board where you get to skip all that makes a hell of a difference to how a person starts their day, so obviously I miss it. However the reverse of the commute was to get off the ship when you had some free time, and that was usually a bit of a headache. Passengers always get priority in going first and if you were tendering offshore, then you could be queuing for some time before you finally made it across, by which point you'd have run out of time and had to get your arse back for napkin folding or something. In a bid to try and maximise our free time ashore, we would try to disguise ourselves as passengers so we could get by Security undetected, which often failed and we were named and shamed in front of the guests.

Another little thing that made me smile was on my weekly schedule. The ACD Gary would always add a little motivational quote that would spur us on and keep us from getting too big for our boots. Things like, 'It's nice to be important but it's important to nice.' For the record I never really viewed myself as being overly important, but the role I held did carry with it an element of importance that made a big difference to the guests having a great time. So to be given a compliment that also curbed an ego from growing too rapidly, was a healthy mentality to try and stick to. It made us feel like we were always growing as individuals, but were also in complete control of maintaining, kind of like a bonsai tree. Plus there were more than enough egos around to be aware of so being an additional diva felt surplus to requirement.

We often got guest entertainers on-board and the occasional odd celebrity, usually bringing with them heavy egos as carry on. Two individuals who were a breath of fresh air by comparison were technically guests, however they were both figures known in the public eye and they had healthy attitudes towards fame and fortune, something that we seemed to have a distinct lack of. Those people were the football legend Welsh/Everton goalkeeper Neville Southall, and one half of the comedy duo cannon and ball, Bobby Ball. He was cruising as a guest to provide moral support for his sons, who were on that week as our guest entertainers, and I believe it was their first time working the cruise ship circuit. How nice is that? It's a perfect example of solid follow through parenting that you don't normally see these days. Mr Ball was incredibly sweet and he wasn't short on giving advice when asked; he was genuinely one of the nicest people to chat with. Mr Southall was equally charming. He and his friends played bingo every single day and he'd always call me over, order me a drink and just want to swap stories and chat. You can't dislike people like that, it's just not possible.

Sitting among such humble and polite individuals who many looked up to sometimes made me question the attitudes and personas of my own superiors. Some of them over the years carried themselves as though they had already made it, and spoke as though the sun peaked from their posteriors. The pomposity of a few of them had me scratching my head, as I had no idea where this arrogance came from or what good it served. They were billy big bollocks on and off stage, but usually in two very disparate identities. For example one of them was the campest northerner I had ever met. His everyday accent sounded like he would have been at home on a stage in Blackpool as part of some tacky cabaret legends tribute show. He was exactly how I would imagine Cilla Black or Vera Duckworth if they were a guy, however when he went on stage he turned into something totally different. He sounded more like a radio DJ from the early 90's, think Harry Enfield and Paul Whitehouse as Smashey and Nicey: *Well a very good evening to you all ladies and gentlemen and welcome to the Oklahoma lounge, are you ready for a good time?! Ho-Ho-Hooo the louder you scream the faster the ride, let's rock!* If you like that kind of thing then no judgement given, for me though I find that style of entertainment utterly cringe worthy.

Another person I used to work with had two very different alter egos. She was an elderly English woman with many years' experience in the entertainment industry. In front of an audience she was prim and proper, courteous and gracious. Her on-stage persona was the sweetest thing I have ever witnessed. It wasn't so sugary that it came out sickly; she found a level of sweetness that is rarely seen and she honed it. Just did a quick google search on sweetest things ever and unfortunately she isn't there. However I did learn that Stevia is about 250 times sweeter than your average table sugar, the Katemfe fruit is around 2,000 times sweeter, but the sweetest thing out there was made in 1996 at Université de Lyon, and is a completely synthesized substance called Lugduname, which is reportedly over 200,000 times sweeter than regular table sugar which is ridiculous!

So yes she was a real sweetheart, and she had a tone of voice whereby when she'd finished speaking, no matter what it was you couldn't help yourself from going, 'aww'. For example: *I was feeling slightly peckish the other week, so I killed the neighbour's cat and made a kitty-cat Fajita.* Aww. One of her trademark phrases was at the end of the night where she would say, "Ladies and gentlemen, that is regrettably the end of this evening's entertainment, but whatever you decide to do for the rest of the night, you enjoy it, and I'll see you all around the ship. Thank you and good night." (Awwww). Then as soon as she was back in the office behind closed doors she was a completely different person. She went so cockney that her legs fell limp, her face scrunched up and the words just fell out of her mouth like hot chips making a quick exit. "Fackin' hell, Sam," she said all cockney like, "this fackin lot had better fack off soon mate I've had just about e-fackin-nuff. I just wanna have an oily rag and duck 'n' dive down the near 'n' far, pig and roast with a pimple and blotch and tumble down the sink to drain the rattle and clank until I'm coals and coke." (Translation – I just want to have a fag and hide down the bar, toast with a scotch and drink to drain the bank until I'm broke). What a lady.

Going out with the show team was always an adventure. One of my favourite places to explore with them was Morocco. We would navigate the twists and turns of the souk market in Agadir, hearing Moroccan traders attempting English accents, proclaiming their items were *"cheap as chips"* and *"luvly jubbly"*. The only thing I ever really went to the souk for was to haggle over the price of bootleg DVDs. I loved Morocco. From Agadir we would go up to Casablanca, then round to Tangier where we could sit at a restaurant on the beach, eat a camel burger and take in the view of the strait of Gibraltar. I remember on one of these occasions, a colleague of mine asked the waiter for a bottle of water. He came back with a cup and saucer and said, "I bring coffee for you?" My colleague was feeling stressed and it showed, as she began to get a little belligerent towards the poor waiter and challenged his intelligence. As she went to move her chair to stand up, the waiter shrieked and the contents of the coffee cup was thrown at her crotch. This provoked my colleague to let out an even louder shriek, but it was cut short when it became apparent that instead of there being hot coffee in the cup, it was actually flower petals. Compared to the ceaseless flow of online videos, where people do tasteless pranks on unsuspecting targets, this was one of the nicest pranks I have seen play out. I like to think that our waiter was emotionally sensitive enough to consider that his prank might help ease my colleagues stress levels, because that is exactly what it did. He'd disarmed the bomb with seconds left on the clock, mission accomplished. If that wasn't his motivation then I guess he was just being a bit of a dick.

One of my hosting highlights was with one of the show girls, as each week we got to host Scattergories up on the open deck. This event was something I always looked forward to because it really helped me to get comfortable on the mic. We held three rounds for the competing teams, all hoping to win that all elusive company branded pen or keyring. I remember the different Scattergories we used because we always used the same ones each week. They were things in the car beginning with S, things in the bedroom beginning with D, and body parts beginning with P. Those last two especially always helped the guests to set the tone of the cruise with regards to how rude they wanted to be. With kids playing in the pool and running around the open deck, I always had to be on form when it came to live censorship. Constant reminders of, *it's a family cruise folks,* fell on deaf ears as answer sheet after answer sheet were filled with smut and filth. The questions were obviously engineered to be suggestively naughty, but some people took their blue humour to new levels of extreme sometimes. I had to make sure to hold the mic close to my chest for fear of them grabbing it from me and blurting out some obscene remark. The experience definitely helped me to get a better handle on reading an audience and at the same time keep them in control.

A lot of the things we had to host had cue cards to read from, which acted as a helpful guide to follow. Usually every time you repeat something you get a little bit better at it the next time round, and in the case of hosting, it could mean that you made up a joke that went down well, so you kept it in and used it every time afterwards. This practice helps you develop an act over time, but if you get to a level where you have it as good as you believe it can get, then you run the risk of getting too comfy with it, and repetition can make it sound like it is being mechanically read from a script. To try and shake things up we used to challenge each other backstage. We would pull random words out of a hat and would then have to go on stage and try to slip those words in somehow. It was particularly funny when my colleagues used those words out of context because they thought they meant something completely different. For example one guy thought the word confectionary meant iron, as in the thing you use to steam your clothes with. As he weaved it confidently into a sentence he thought made perfect sense, you could virtually see a Mexican wave of eyebrows raising.

Now and again, I would help out the kids' hosts with some of their activities, like setting up Mario Kart on the main stage projector screen, and running tournaments which of course I dominated! Or sometimes I would play the evil pirate who would occasionally pop up and chase them around the ship, as they attempted to solve riddles that had been easily hidden, and you can keep your paedophile jokes to yourself as playing the villain is so much fun. One particular life-long dream of mine is to one day play the character Bill Sykes or Fagin from the musical Oliver as I just think that would be amazing. Eliciting boos and screams from an audience is such a satisfyingly warm and fuzzy feeling and is definitely up there with getting laughs.

I remember the first time a couple of kids came running up to me, pen and paper in hand, and asked me for my autograph. To be quite honest I was humbled by this request, as I momentarily pondered what kind of positive influential impact I was having on these kids as an entertainer. The moment was however short lived because as soon as I had finished writing them a short inspirational message of hope and encouragement, they went straight to a barman and asked for his John Hancock as well. It turned out that they were on a scavenger hunt and needed 'autographs' from somebody working in each department on-board. Oh well. Knowing my luck, if I ever do amount to anything, my fictional mad cap fans will probably go straight past me at the table and go grab a signature from a security guard or staff member instead.

Sitting quite high up in the ranks of my favourite things are the sporting achievements I accrued over the years I spent at sea. They are made all the more special because I achieved them on a moving ship which is no easy feat! My humble brags include being undefeated at giant Jenga up on the open deck, a record I achieved by using two discarded pieces as a rudimentary hammer and chisel, to carefully chip away at the more stubborn pieces. When the structure began to tower over us as the ship swayed, it became an accident waiting to happen and small children had to be kept away for fear of crushing them. Luckily it never toppled on my go so I have pathetically clung to the title of giant Jenga champ all these years.

Another sport I got rather good at was table tennis. In all my years spent at sea I never was fortunate enough to work on a ship where the table was indoors, instead it would be up on deck and a game could sometimes be heavily influenced by the wind. I'm not the best player out there, but I'm certainly not terrible. In fact I would say that out of all the sports I play it's the one I'm the most consistently inconsistent at. It's totally psychological I swear, because when I'm having a bad game I'm absolutely shocking and there is no morale I can scrape together, and no dignity I can salvage. When I'm good and able to hold my own I feel like fictional ping pong hero Forest Gump. The most epic game I ever had was against a semi-professional Russian guest. The wind was blowing a bit but the pair of us had a rally that equalled that which you might see on TV. We must've both been standing at least a meter and a half away from the table on both sides as we delivered forearm smash after smash at each other. The intensity of the battle between us drew a crowd of guests to the table, and they cheered us on, making the action feel even more spectacular. We played old table tennis rules, five serves each, first to 21, and it went to sudden death. In the end I lost 29 to 27, but to this day it was the most amazing game I've ever played because my opponent was so good he brought out the very best in me.

One game we played a lot down in the crew bar after work was darts, and our game of choice was Killer. This is a great game to play because there's no quick maths involved, and people at all levels of skill can enjoy the game as well. The idea is that you throw a single dart at the board with your weaker hand, and whatever you land on becomes your designated number. Then you each take turns at trying to hit your number five times with your chosen hand. Once you achieve this you are a killer, and can now start going for other people's numbers. The amount of times they have hit their own number, is the amount of lives they have. So for example if their number is nineteen and they have hit it four times, when it's your turn you can knock them out of the game by hitting a treble and single nineteen. The game can get very competitive very quickly, as rivalries can be forged, friendships can be broken, bets can be taken and in my case, money can be lost. I did however honourably win some of it back over time, and I bought my own tungsten darts with gyro flights in Gibraltar. I had gone into the sport a complete novice but by contract's end, was the proud recipient of a mock Most Improved Player of the Year award, and as soon as I got home I got a dartboard of my own and hung it in the garage.

Golfing on-board can come in many different forms. If you're on a really massive, expensive ship then they might have a state of the art golfing simulator. On some other ships they might offer a mini golf course or a cage where you can practice your long drive. I once heard tale of a ship where you could smack compressed balls of fish food off the back deck into the ocean, how cool is that!? If you didn't have any of the above then it was usually some crappy self-returning putting matt or something along those lines. On one ship I used to make my own miniature golf courses using gaffer tape on the floor, and penalised people a stroke for going outside the lines. One day I had nobody turn up to the event so I didn't bother making a course. Instead I set up the putt-returner as far away as was physically possible. It was quite a small ship and the beam (width) was only 22 metres, so once I had successfully completed that challenge I moved into the guest cabin corridor to attempt a new personal best. The total length of the ship was around 157m, and the current Guinness world record is 120m. This was obviously achieved on a real golf course and the guy who did it, really hit it with some force. If you watch his attempt he gets some pretty good air and the ball curls quite a bit on the green towards the end. I was unable to whack the crap out of my ball for fear of breaking something or someone, and I only had the width of the corridor to work with so it regularly bounced off the walls like when you go bowling and the kids have the barriers up. There were virtually no guests on-board so I was free to make many uninterrupted attempts, my only worry was if an elderly guest should unexpectedly emerge from their room, or a senior officer should come along and spoil my fun. Luckily they didn't, but when I think back to that glorious putt it doesn't sit in my mind as particularly graceful. It bounced off the walls and over metal floor coverings at quite some speed. I estimate the distance was somewhere over the 50m mark, and when it finally crawled up the ramp and neatly slotted into the hole I was overjoyed. I leapt into the air and looked around to see if there was anyone else that I could share my elation with. The single greatest sporting moment I ever truly nailed in my history was sadly witnessed by no-one. Never have I ever experienced such a rapid come down from such a massive high.

When guests did turn up to events however, it would usually be the same people every time. They would take it so seriously that it would take the fun out of the game and they would all insist that the rules they used were the rules everyone played by. These people never got off the ship and would pride themselves on being the guest at the end of the cruise with the most trophies or keyrings. They were so competitive that they would go up against children and show no mercy. A lot of these children were often spoilt and would leave in floods of tears because they couldn't have a prize. Trying to generate fun for the guests under these circumstances wasn't exactly one of my favourite things, I just think it's rather funny how much people care about taking home a company-branded pen.

One woman was so desperate to win a prize during an evening gameshow, that she really demonstrated the dangers of being overly competitive. In one section of the show, a prize would be given to the first person to reach the stage, tap the host on the shoulder and give the correct answer to a question. Without any hesitation this woman bolted straight through the audience, hurdling through tables and chairs as she went. Unfortunately she tripped and fell face first through a glass table. If you ever find yourself in this situation, let this story be a warning to all of you, and know that a company branded pen or keyring really isn't all that worth it.

I just realised that I've included a story about a woman who could have been severely injured at the end of a chapter all about my favourite things, no less. So what kind of proverbial spin can I put to round off this chapter? How about - a company branded pen or keyring was one of her favourite things, but you can't always get what you want? Or look before you leap? How about, all that glitters is not gold? Take your pick...

Chapter 9

Incredibly Exciting, Inciting Incidents

I wanted to dedicate this chapter to the types of stories that are wholly indicative of what ship life can be like. If you love your drama then you'll find there is no shortage of it with ship life. I think it's fair to say that it if it weren't for the guests, life on-board might actually be quite peaceful. We had it all, everything a good soap opera needs. An open buffet of arguments, an engine room of complaints, and a medical room constantly coping with injuries, emergencies, and even deaths. We had to stay sharp at all times and on top of the never ending drills we had to endure, sometimes the safety officer would chuck the additional bomb scare into the mix. For this, all crew members need to check every nook and cranny of the ship, searching high and low for a couple of hidden fake bombs. On one occasion I actually found one in my room, I think the safety officer might not have liked me on that ship and may have been hinting it slightly.

The petty squabbles I used to have with guests would make your head spin. For example I remember going up to the sports deck to start my basketball event to find a woman sunbathing nude slap bang in the middle of the court. She had very cheekily lifted up the netting and slipped her sun bed inside. I approached with extreme caution and let her know that I was about to start an event, so would she please mind moving to the open deck. Of course she wasn't happy and her argument was: "That's not fair. I was here first." I replied, "You can sunbathe anywhere, but this is the only place on-board anyone can play basketball." She was reluctant to move even though she hadn't exactly chosen the best of places to sunbathe - the netting cast its shadow across her body and she was starting to look a bit like Pinhead from the film Hell Raiser. When I pointed this out to her she eventually moved. Then my event was able to finally go ahead, and it was the worst one I ever hosted. Rowdy teenagers all getting lairy with one another, pushing, shoving, kicking, biting and punching. It was only a small court, so I had to rotate games so everyone had a chance to play. Some of the lads who were waiting impatiently outside the court for their game did something I will never forget. The exact details are unclear to me as I was refereeing at the time, but basically they were doing dares, and it went so far that one lad actually got peer pressured into hanging off the side of the ship on a lighting fixture. I kid you not! When

I confronted the idiot child about what he had just done, I made sure that I instilled the fear in him that would ensure he'd never do it again. I told him that if he fell from that height he'd be knocked out cold, break every bone in his body, and be almost impossible to find. He didn't believe me and started acting tough in front of his so-called friends, so I lied about there being sharks in the water and he went white as a ghost, and he promised never to do it again. Then we resumed play and another kid split his head open on the floor, flippin' typical.

Some ships are able to offer suites with balconies to the guests. Unfortunately I never personally got to experience the pleasure of waking up and going out on to the balcony for a morning stretch whilst at sea. I imagine this must be one of the most serene ways to settle into the day, although for one guest it was unfortunately quite the opposite. They had woken up feeling rather hung over and crawled from bed to balcony, only to find themselves faced not with the ocean, but another ship leaving the port, and all its guests out on deck waving goodbye to us. Oh, and they were butt naked ... the hungover guest, that is, not the waving guests ... that would've been extremely weird, although not unheard of, as there are a number of cruise companies out there that offer nudist charter holidays. I wouldn't worry about booking a cruise and not realising it was a nudist week, that's virtually impossible. It's not impossible however for a person to give birth on-board without having known they were even pregnant. I have no idea how, but this happened to a lady once on-board, and she ended up naming her child Destiny, after the ship. Thank god it wasn't something like Queen Mary or Prince Albert. The papers got a hold of the story, and the headline read, 'Destiny's Child'. Awww.

One rather dramatic problem inexperienced cruisers face is cabin fever. This is the term given for when a person experiences a claustrophobic reaction from being stuck indoors for extended periods of time. They display symptoms of extreme irritability, anxiety and restlessness. Their erratic and unpredictable behaviour is cause for concern as they could do damage to themselves and others. Some people just can't handle the idea of being stuck on a ship in the middle of the ocean, so madness often follows. One guest hadn't exactly been on-board all that long, but he went bat shit crazy within a few hours of being at sea. He made his way down to crew areas and barricaded himself in the laundry room with sun loungers and clothes rails. When security came down to handle the situation, they were met with a volley of clothes hangers, tables and chairs. When they were finally able to tackle the man to floor, he was handcuffed and thrown in the brig, and rightly so!

Security are some of the toughest mother fuckers out there, and a big portion of them are Nepalese Gurkhas who are known for being utterly fearless. They love to recite a quote which comes from former Indian Army Chief of Staff Field Marshall (what a title) Sam Manekshaw, which is: *If a man says he's not afraid of dying, he's either lying or a Gurkha.* The epaulettes on their shoulders display a pair of Khukuri daggers which are a Gurkha's signature weapon of choice, but they do not carry them around the ship because truthfully these guys do not need weapons, their hands will do the job just fine. Furthermore, higher-ups worry that potentially dangerous passengers might get their hands on them. So for this reason most ships do not stash a hidden supply of weapons on-board, but this is not a blanket statement as some ships employ their own private security. Like in the case of the MSC Melody cruise ship in 2009, which was attacked by Somalian pirates a few hundred miles south of the Seychelles. As the pirates tried to scale the vessel, guests frantically threw tables and chairs down at their attackers to try and knock them into the water. The pirates managed to get a few shots off from their AK-47s, but failed to board the ship because when security arrived, luckily they too had guns. I was on a ship around that area the year before on a smaller vessel, and after I'd read that story and watched the film Captain Phillips, I often wondered how I would have coped in that situation, or how I would have dealt with possibly being kidnapped and held for ransom. I'd like to think that I would have remained an unbreakable spirit, and shown an unshakeable stoicism in the face of my captors. Though it is likely that I would have gone kicking and screaming, probably yelling things like, *Please, it's my first week! I'm nobody I'm just a Bingo caller. I'M JUST A BINGO CALLERRRR!!!*

As I mentioned earlier a big part of my day was having to socialise with the guests. It was a pretty strange thing at first to have to go up to people and just say, "Hey guys! How you all doing? Mind if I join you?" It's not really common practice anywhere in the real world, but on a ship it's slightly more normal. The way my bosses sold it to me was that because we were one of the faces of the ship's entertainment, the guests would be delighted to be seen sitting next to one of us. Like it somehow made them feel special above everyone else, or that they had been the lucky winners of some sad competition. But these guests hadn't entered any competitions, they were just regular folks sitting down enjoying each other's company, so sometimes they didn't want to me to join them, and replied to my *mind if I join you?* with, *Nah you're alright mate.* I'll be honest that stung at first, but I got through it and developed thicker skin over time. Why should they want me to sit down? I was nobody. Why should you read this memoir? I'm still nobody. But looking back I see it as being as annoying as cold calling or door to door sales, but it's probably even worse because I didn't even have anything to sell. Essentially I'm going up to people to ask if I can break up their private conversations, and get them to talk about something else that I can join in with. At first I only ever used to go up to happy, chatty tables because they looked like the most fun to be a part of, and the easiest to approach. This was clearly a mistake because they were already having a good time, and they didn't need me to go over there to cheer them up or make them feel 'special'. So I decided that I would try to meet the kind of people who looked like they could do with an ice breaker, the ones who were sitting in complete silence, staring out the window with their arms crossed. They were always more than happy for someone to come and sit with them, desperate even. Anything to help them forget how bored of the other person they had become. This logic is definitely not fool proof as sometimes the look on people's faces can quite literally read *fuck off*. It's not hard to spot, and you're a damn fool if you think 'be the change that you wish to see in the world' should be applied in this kind of situation. Sorry, Mahatma Ghandi.

On one occasion I was doing my rounds and approached a couple in their mid to late 60s who fit this description. When I asked if I could join them the woman eagerly grabbed my arm and pulled me straight down into an empty seat right beside her. The man looked at me and said nothing. He didn't give much away so it was kind of difficult to read the situation. The woman was really nice and very chatty, but she asked me a flood of questions and seemed very excitable. I kept trying to swing it round so that I could keep the conversation flowing both ways, but it became painfully clear to me quite soon after sitting down, that the conversation was only being exchanged between the two of us, so I tried to throw the man a couple of direct questions. His answers were short and almost dismissive, so I took the hint and wrapped things up so I could leave, as I sensed he didn't really appreciate my being there. Later on that evening my boss called me into his office to have a private word. He said, "Sam have you said or done anything to anyone tonight that might have upset or offended them in any way?" I thought about it for a moment before confidently replying, "No … ..why, what's happened?" He said, "Because I've just had a call from reception who told me they've had a complaint against you from a guest … any idea who that might be from?" I honestly had no idea who had complained, what I might have said or done to offend anyone so I spoke up. "I've got absolutely no idea, what on earth did I do?" My boss studied me for a moment to look for any body language that might have suggested I wasn't telling the truth, and then said, "There was a man down at reception just now, who said that you sat with them for a drink and you were hitting on his wife right in front of him," (*WHAT THE HELL* ran through my mind) "he said that they are staying for two weeks and he doesn't want to see you again AND they have a cruise booked later this year on another ship and if you're on it, he won't be stepping foot on-board." I told my boss exactly what happened. He studied me again for any nervous tells or signs of dishonesty, then he relaxed a bit and said, "Okay, so the mans an idiot then." I breathed a sigh of relief and was advised to just steer clear of him. A week went by and I hadn't seen the couple all that much, I think I may have dodged them on purpose once or twice but that's it. Then one evening out of nowhere the man came up to me and asked for a quiet word. He said that he wanted to apologise for putting in the complaint against me because he admitted that he was wrong. He'd been watching me all week and seen me going up to other couples and chatting with them in the same manner I sat with him and his wife. He also confessed that his partner was a widow when he'd met her, and so now they were a couple of newly-weds. He was sincerely sorry because he admitted that he was probably a little overprotective of her, and he bought me a drink to bury the hatchet. So in the case of this story, all's well that ends well, as later that night I made love to his wife.

… I'm joking!

One of the worst times I ever had dealing with a constant influx of guest complaints was when a sister ship broke down. It was scheduled to arrive in port the day after us, but due to an engine failure was unable to make the trip. So our ship had to stay an extra day in port to make sure the company were able to receive the new guests flying in, and who were expecting to board the ship they had booked. Taking full advantage of the overnight opportunity, myself and a few others headed out for a night on the town. So the next morning I was feeling rather worse for wear, and over a thousand angry guests turned up on the quayside without a ship to board. The hardest thing was to arrange last minute hotels for all the guests, whilst at the same time deal with constant complaints. Angry face after angry face steamed up to me demanding answers, and I was hanging out my arse the whole time barely holding it together. I tried to calm them down as best I could, jokingly remarking that the situation wasn't that bad, and worse things have happened at sea. Which was rubbing salt in the wound a bit as they would have of course liked to have been at sea. But it's totally true! Worse things have happened at sea! They should've been thanking us for not taking them with us, as they were probably much safer to stay on dry land. They might have to face fires, deal with storms, listen to terrible jokes, and in the most extreme cases, death. I mentioned earlier in the book that I used to live opposite the ship's morgue, which was where we kept the dead bodies, and reading it back like that made it sound pretty sinister, like we were all part of some twisted secret evil plan to rid the world of cruisers, like that movie Hostel, which targeted backpackers instead.

I only heard of people dying on-board a few times. Probably the most upsetting was a fellow crew member. During an emergency crew drill one day, a maintenance man tried to pass through a watertight door as it was slowly closing automatically. Water tight doors are huge thick steel doors, which close in case of an emergency when the ship takes on water. When they are closed they can prevent the ship from sinking, as they prevent water travelling from one compartment to another, and they are usually situated down on the lower decks of the ship like the engine room. So, this guy went to step through the door and he tripped and got stuck in an instant. The outcome was as horrifying as you can imagine, and to ensure that no crew would ever attempt to make the same mistake ever again, a picture of the man's bloody boiler suit was posted next to every watertight door … chilling.

We used to get quite a lot of repeat cruisers on-board who became like family to us sometimes. Seeing them walk up the quay was always uplifting as it was good to see a familiar face among the swarms of first timers. We had this old guy called Ron who used to cruise with us every other month; he never cruised with any company except ours. He knew everyone's name in our department, and for some of us he used to bring the odd home comforts with him as well. For my boss it was a bottle of Ribena, for one of my colleagues it was always a bunch of melted curly wurlys, and for me, my staple diet of nice n' spicy nik naks. Ron always travelled alone and unfortunately had a really bad case of arthritis. He smoked a lot so his fingernails were a dark yellowy colour, and because of his arthritis his hands were like misshapen hooks. He had no family or significant others in his life, so he put all his time and energy into us as a team. To him, we were his family, and for any of us that knew Ron, seeing him felt like a family member returning to visit. I remember him regularly showing up at the gangway always looking rather dishevelled, so I'd take his suitcase for him and walk him to his cabin. He carried two things on him at all times: a comb in his front pocket and a seat ring. I never pried into his personal life or discussed with him in detail his health complaints, he always just wanted to chat shit and joke about. He had a really cheeky sense of humour, was always upbeat, and even though he was in constant pain, he never moaned or complained about anything. I learnt a lot from Ron during my time over the contract, and I was sad to hear of his death which happened on another one of our ships. I heard he passed away up on the Lido deck whilst eating dinner, and shortly after he departed, his bowels released. The guests on the tables around him quickly up and left as the smell was apparently unbearable. Ron loved his toilet humour so it was almost a fitting end for him. RIP Ron, I hope in heaven they have triple ply as standard and clouds so soft to sit on they don't need seat rings, buddy.

Ron's death was not the only guest death I heard of at sea. It is normal for news to travel at breakneck speed whenever something goes wrong, but in the case of these following deaths, their stories circulated quickly because of the imagery they leave in our brains. Death is a tricky subject to make light of, but I'm pretty sure if you've read this far and not been offended by anything, then the next two paragraphs should be no problem for you.

There was a guy who died on the toilet whilst on-board. He was apparently really constipated and his neighbours could testify to this as they had heard his struggles from nearby. When the doctor arrived on the scene the man was found dead on the floor in the foetal position. In the toilet bowl there was a single solitary nugget, but there was an unfortunate amount of excrement on the bathroom floor as well. I cannot remember exactly how he died, might have been a heart attack, or it could have been an embolism popped in his brain, but there was one other thing about the man's departure that leaves a lasting impression in my mind, and that was his lockjaw. His face clearly showed in alarming detail his final struggle. Apparently the doctor had to use the man's belt which she tied around his head and yanked on it hard to shut the man's jaw close.

Another man on a different occasion was rushed to the medical room because he was going into cardiac arrest, and it was later discovered that he had taken more than the recommended dosage for Viagra. Whilst C.P.R was underway, a strange anomaly occurred. For each and every time the doctor completed a chest compression, the man's penis flexed up toward his belly button. The sheer sight of it had the staff captain and security guard present in pieces, so the doctor had to ask them to leave. Later when the man was pronounced dead, his wife was trying to retrieve the wedding ring from his hand perhaps a little too hastily. Her initial thought to get it back was to saw off the finger. The man had literally just died and this wife of his wasn't wasting any time trying to get every penny she could out of the poor bugger. The Doctor took a moment to process what she'd just heard, and then calmly suggested using Vaseline instead, which the wife shrugged and said was, "Okay, I suppose."

There aren't many incidents that occur on-board that are kept secret for long. Being in a place where gossip is practically a second form of currency, the walls all have ears and anyone's business is anyone's business.

Chapter 10

Reintegrating with Reality

My first cruise contract was coming to an end and not a moment too soon. I had extended a six-month contract into a ten month one and was now definitely ready to go home.

It was the longest contract on any ship I ever did which was a hell of an introduction to ship life. There was a lot to process and ropes to learn, a lot of friends made and experiences gained. I worked seven days a week for the entirety of that contract and I only had one sick day the whole time, and I still had to work on it! Not that I didn't chose to, that's for sure. There I was minding my own business down in my cabin, tucked up safe and secure in bed with a cough and runny nose that wouldn't quit. Then I hear that piercingly loud, gut-bustingly obnoxious telephone ring. My boss was freaking out because in my absence he was short of staff to help him run his gameshow smoothly. He was soon to start hosting Deal or no Deal, and had to have eighteen guests on stage with him. So he needed me for the most important role of all. To be a moving mic stand and help to capture the pearls of wisdom each contestant offered when it comes to opening a box and hoping to blind luck. I slid out of bed and into my suit hating everyone. I got up there just as the show had to start, and I coughed and spluttered my way through the whole show.

I really hate the concept of Deal or no Deal as it's not based on anything except blind dumb luck. There's no strategy or way you could ever really prepare yourself to win, you just roll with it. It's probably the worst gameshow of all time in my opinion. The only thing that makes the game exciting to watch is the drama around the unknown possibility of whether or not someone will be walking away with a cash prize somewhere between one million and one pound. Obviously we didn't have huge cash sums to part with on the ship, so we went with a different scale. Anywhere between 25 quid and a penny. You're probably thinking, *but then the show surely must've been shit!* and right you are! However, a big factor of the show's entertainment rests on the shoulders of the contestants. We had bad shows in the past because we had some really boring contestants in the hot seat, so we did what we had to do in the name of entertainment and decided to rig it. Underneath one of the eighteen chairs that our potential contestants sat on, we hid a playing card, and whoever sat in that seat would be in the show. We always made sure that someone we knew was good for a laugh was sitting in that chair so - problem solved. We also didn't have a banker, instead we had an old red rotary phone on the table which wasn't even plugged in, and the sound guy would play a sound clip of a phone ringing, genius right? Everyone knew that the host was of course not on the phone to anyone, but that just made it funnier. In terms of my role during all this I could be doing one of three things: the power point operator, the moving mic stand, or the prize showcaser. This was one of my favourite roles to play early on because it was a chance for me to display some of my burgeoning comedic talents. Basically the banker would 'call up' mid-game, and after a bit of banter the host would hang up and say the banker would like to offer you whatever, and then I'd come on presenting the prize, but it was never what the audience expected to see. Not having money for the imaginary banker to barter with, we had to be pretty creative with our prizes. So there would be prizes like "A brand new caaaaaaar!" then I'd bring out a small fruit and veg carving on a plate from an earlier demonstration. "The banker would like to offer you today's ice carving" then I'd come on carrying two pint glasses of water, claiming that the walk-in freezer was broken, and that this was all I could salvage. The last prize I can remember is, "A free cruise ... brochure" and on I'd skip showing off a shiny catalogue of cruises, only to then be publicly criticized again because it was out of date.

The role was fun to play as it broke up the mundanity of the show, and whoever had the role would always have the audience in hysterics ... probably because the rest of the show was so dull.

My cruise director, Stewart used to have this speech that he gave at the end of the final show on the last night of the cruise. It was something I heard repeated many, many times, but towards the end of the contract it only became more poignant. He would basically say something that went as follows:

"Ladies and Gentlemen, each night you come in here and shower us with praise for the shows we put on, and whilst we appreciate it, we are here doing a job designed to receive applause. So I'd like to take this opportunity to remind you of all the other staff who work tirelessly to ensure you have a wonderful cruise, and who don't get applauded. Here on-board they are the unsung heroes, so let's hear it for them. They are your bar staff! (*applause*) Your waiters! (*applause*) Your housekeepers! (*you get the idea*). I just want to say that there are over 30 different nationalities on-board, all working hard seven days a week. They all live and work in this environment together peacefully, and if we can do that at sea, ladies and gentlemen, well then why can't we do it in the real world?"

Following those rousing final words the audience would stand and cheer, raise their glasses and clap. This was the kind of end to a week spent in their company that you would hope to see I suppose. There was more to the speech than that but I just wanted to focus on that portion of it in particular. I must've heard it at least a hundred times, and after a while the words began to lose their impact, but thinking of home as it drew ever closer, the words took root in me once again as they had done the first time I'd heard them. What came to mind was the thought of London, where there is a place for everyone, and everyone comes from most places. I thought of people I'm ashamed to know who think the world owes them a living, and as they struggle with their own existence they blame their failures on others and on immigration. I thought of a time when I was in central London, and from across a busy road I saw a gnarly looking homeless man go up to a young Chinese couple taking pictures and ask them for a *faaag*. They weren't smoking, and he got up quite close in their personal space which made the pair of them jump out their skins. They apologised profusely for not having a cigarette and were practically cowering in fear. In response the homeless man spat of them and screamed, "You've got no idea, do ya! No cares or worries in life! Just taking money off your daddy. Ya ain't got a clue how hard life is!" He didn't appear to be drunk, which even if he was is no excuse, but something about this memory made me think about my own past, present and future. Up until this point I could see myself in the shoes of the Chinese couple. Young, innocent, inexperienced and with hardly any cares or worries to write home about. The homeless man came in as a contrasting thought, that if I ever came to expect anything from anyone moving forward, then my whole experience from my first contract would have been a total waste of time. No matter what is going wrong for you in your own life, it's inexcusable to take your anger out on others. It was time to start giving again, show thanks and appreciation for all that I was lucky enough to have. I thought of my parents. How they had raised three children and helped put me on the path to where I was now. I felt as though I owed them a huge debt for the lessons I'd learnt from them, and gratitude for the experiences they'd afforded me. I thought how much money they had spent on me since I'd been born, and how little had I given back. Could I have shown more love and appreciation towards them? Probably. At the age of nineteen I realised that the decision to start working on cruise ships was about as much my idea as it was my parents'. They wanted me to go for my own benefit, and to get shot of me for theirs as well. And if I was in their shoes, I think I probably would have done the same thing.

There was a run of consistently good crowds on-board in the build up towards the end of the contract, so when the big day came around where myself and the team finally got to fly back home, it was even harder for us all to say goodbye and the quayside was awash with tears. The new guys were in place and all set to take over so all that was left to do was to get our arses to the airport and back to Blighty.

When I stepped off the plane at Heathrow, I drew in a deep breath of air and was satisfyingly convinced that I had landed in the right country. It wasn't long until I met my parents and sister who had come to pick me up (more tears surprise surprise, not from me ... again it was all mother), but I remember the thing I was most excited for was to see was my dog. There isn't a being on this planet that can make you feel like you were more sorely missed than a dog. When a dog has been home alone all day they go crazy when they hear keys jangle in the lock. So in my mind I could see my ecstatic dog doing backflips in anticipation for my long-awaited return. When I got to the front door, I knelt down and could see the dog's tail waving frantically through the translucent glass, and when I opened it, I threw my arms wide and called out, "*Suzi!*" She looked up at me for less than a second, sneezed, and then squeezed between my legs to go to my mum and dad.

Now ... I loved that damn dog with all my heart. I fed and watered her, gave her medicine, brushed her teeth occasionally, and took her for long muddy walks round the countryside, then gave her a nice soapy scrub down and rinsed her off in the bath. So for her to go straight to my parents was a bit heart-breaking.

My mum has this ability to sometimes convey things of little to no importance in a way that makes it sound catastrophic, so her choice of language can at times be open to different interpretations. For example one morning she burst in my room yelling, "Suzi's breaking her neck outside!" My friend Darren, who was staying round on a sleepover at the time (this is when we were of an age when it was still socially acceptable to call them sleepovers) looked at me with panic in his eyes and said, "Did she say breaking her neck or broken?" I was as clueless as he was because I was still rubbing the sleep out my eyes. So without another word we raced down to the garden to see the dog running around after the ball like she was jacked up on cocaine. I said "For god's sake, Mum, you had us really worried then! We both thought the dog had just died!"

Anyway, my dog totally ignoring me after my ten-month absence wasn't the immediate response I was hoping for, but after ten or so minutes she seemed to remember my scent and cautiously began to lick the back of my hand. Then later on that evening, she was all cozied up next to me on the couch. Now I felt like I truly was back home.

It's a funny thing returning home after any extended period of time. If you go away on holiday for two weeks you won't exactly come home to a dystopian future or an apocalyptic nightmare, but after ten months I noticed a few things had changed. For instance when I left home, Facebook and YouTube had just about started, and by the time I had come back their popularity had grown exponentially. I was away trying to learn how to be a better entertainer, to gain more understanding of how to work a live audience and communicate more effectively towards them. But when I came back and decided to re-join society in the 'real world' from the bubble I had been in, that world had shifted and now everyone was trying to work the webcam. I was thrown into a land of constant connectivity and interaction via social media, it was something I felt totally unprepared for. I felt how I imagine my nan feels when I try to explain how to work the DVD player, only now DVDs were now practically a thing of the past, so all those lessons I'd given were a complete waste of time. Everyone was banging on about Blu-ray this and Blu-ray that. Meanwhile I was standing there screaming, *What the fuck is Blu-ray!? What the hell is a hashtag?!*

I felt like Shy Stallone as John Spartan in Demolition man. Cryogenically frozen then re-animated three decades later, and unable to grasp the concept of how to use the three seashells to wipe my own arse. If I'd have been more in tune with the fashion trends when I left, then I might have been able to recognise what was now hot and what was not, but truth be told my grasp fashion has always been a constant struggle. I was behind with the news, celebrity gossip, sports, everything! I was a tourist in my own country. So, in a bid to catch up with all that was current, I went to my local with a few mates for a ceremonial wagging of the chins. As we sat round the table they all whipped out super swanky touchscreen smartphones. I was still dicking about with a clunky pay as you go dumb manual phone. So when I asked them about their new models they overwhelmed me by showing apps that had revolutionised the way we get children to sit still and be quiet. For some reason I seem to remember a game called 'chicken slap', which was as simple a game as it sounds. Whilst my head was spinning from all this new Hi-tech gadgetry, I lit up a cigarette right there inside the bar. As I took in that first satisfying drag I saw the jaws of those around me drop to the floor in shock. They looked at me as if I had just dropkicked an old lady in the head. *Mate ... don't you know you can't smoke inside pubs no more?* The news hit me like a freight train to the stomach. I had only been an indoor smoking patron of the pub for one measly year, and now that right had been taken away from me. It was okay on ships still, but the news of the smoking ban somehow hadn't reached me. As I tried to deal with this new blow to the system, I heard a camera shutter click. Then before I knew it, I was slapped on the internet, fag in hand, to be named, shamed and hash tagged. It was like I'd landed on earth in the future and it had been taken over by apes. Except they weren't apes at all. It was a planet of the frapes!

My friend's perception of a life at sea was a bit on the naïve side, and that was fine because I was the same before I'd gone and found out for myself. They assumed that all my time working away had been a combination of Butlins, the Love Boat, the Titanic and swabbing a non-existent poop deck. I say non-existent, only because what a poop deck is and what my friends believe a poop deck to be, are two totally different things. It is not a deck which is completely over-run with human excrement as one might think, but anticlimactically, it means the roof of a cabin built at the aft which forms part of the superstructure of the ship. Poop comes from the French word for stern, which is poupe, or from Latin, puppis. So basically re-worded, it means stern deck. And there you have it! You'll have many moments of glory from this day forth correcting people on what a poop deck technically is.

As I mentioned before, my friends thought I was now of course gay, and that I was now a seamen who loved all types of seamen. The jokes kept on coming in relentlessly but I managed to keep them at bay by admitting that yes, I did have a lot of homosexual co-workers, but that there were also a lot of very attractive female dancer types too, and thanks to the lack of heterosexual competition, it meant that I was cock of the walk. They pressed me on that almost immediately. "So if you was the only straight one, how many birds did you shag?" I'm only a kiss and tell sort of guy when it's private with a couple of my closest friends, but when the group starts asking that's when I tend to clam up. I told them the story of the Hungarian singer, whom unlocked my chastity belt with a skeleton key and stoleth my virginity plates. They just wanted more stories of that kind and didn't really care to hear much of anything else (lads, ey!), but then I was left with only one other romantic entanglement worthy of regaling.

There was this pretty young blonde girl who out of all the guests was 'stunner of the week' and absolutely my cup of tea. She had been a Miss Leicester pageant winner and smelled like pick n' mix. Strictly speaking, intimate relations with guests is a no-no and punishable by immediate dismissal, but that's only if you get caught. A colleague sharply reminded me that PDA (public display of affection) was highly unprofessional and that we needed to stop. The girl was on-board with her friend and her friend's parents, so the absence of pressure from an overbearing father staring me down was something of a relief. We got pretty chummy throughout the week, and on the last night of the cruise I noticed she was a bit sun burnt on her shoulders so I suggested she slap some Aloe Vera on them. She said she didn't have any, so I said I had some down in my cabin and she could use it if she liked… nudge nudge, wink wink. She couldn't go back to her cabin as her friend would be there, so I had to make arrangements for my room to be empty. In the past when couples have been unable to secure a private room, they would resort to places like the lifeboat or even the service elevator, but I wasn't about to take that kind of risk. We arranged to meet up after I'd finished work, I told her to meet me on the staircase by deck one aft at 12:00 just opposite the doctor's office. If I'd have taken her there myself it might have looked too obvious, so I thought it best to have her meet me close to my room to avoid any suspicion. When we finally met up it had the intense thrill of a covert operation and the danger of some kind of shady drug deal. The risk of being found out got my heart rate going, and even though I only had a short distance to escort her, I was still shitting it on the inside. We managed to avoid detection from the security guards, and the mission to make it to my cabin was complete. Once inside she made herself at home and looked at the photographs on my wall for a bit, whilst I took a moment to regulate my heart rate because I was both nervous, relieved and excited. When I calmed down I gave her the ten second tour. Which is all the time it takes to show someone around your cabin. The mood in my cabin was far more pleasant than the first time I had had sex, for one thing my roommate wasn't sitting there playing video games, and also I was sober as a judge. I leaned across her to the shelf on the wall and picked up the bottle of Aloe Vera. She said, "Oh yeah thanks, I'd nearly forgotten about that." I hadn't. I knew all too well that the application of after-sun lotion is crucial for rehydrating sun burnt skin. Helping to repair the skin by cooling it down and locking in lost moisture. Had I verbalised that information at the time then she might have lost even more moisture, but I didn't. I held back. She then slipped the dress off her shoulders, held her hair up and turned around. I took my cue and got stuck in, gently of course. This is sensitive skin I'm dealing with after all. As I liberally lotioned the lower part of her back, I slowly grew the courage to inch my way up to her shoulders for a massage. Once I'd given her back a sensual once over, she turned to face me and slipped the dress down a little further. I'm actually starting to understand why people read erotic novels. This is hot stuff! Unfortunately, I'm not an erotic novelist, and don't feel comfortable going into every sordid detail. From that point of the story I assume you can connect the dots and fill out the paint by numbers without the need for any more detail, but if you must know, she did have cracking tits.

I was a bit older than her so I felt the need to be slightly more dominant, and it was her first time so I was treading a fine line between being gentle with her and being a passionate man-beast wildling. Quite different to the Hungarian girl who was several years older than myself and definitely took the reins that evening.

Pretty soon my mates were getting sick and tired of hearing me telling tall tales from the sea, and as I wasn't working and had now been severely affected by the travel bug, I was itching to get back out there.

One of my colleagues who joined the ship late into my first contract had come from a different cruise line on his previous contract. He said that if I was interested in working for another company he would put in a good word for me. He was true to his word and hooked me up with someone to get in touch with, who interviewed me over the phone and offered me a job. Having all my sea safety training certificates really helped speed up the process, but I had to head back to Harley Street for a few jabs as we would be going to some pretty out of the way places.

I was home for a period no longer than two weeks and hadn't even fully unpacked from my last contract before I was gearing up and heading back out again, this time to work on a much smaller ship, with far fewer people, but a far greater itinerary.

Whilst I readied my bags for yet another adventure, and tried my hardest to ignore my mother's incessant wailing, my brother entered the room and said, "When you gonna get a proper job, Sam?" which took me right back to the question I'd previously been asked by the guests during my contract, *What do you do for a real job?*

"Proper job?" I said, "Ha! You wouldn't last a week!"